EMBRACE YOUR CROWN

DON'T LET THE VOICES DISTRACT YOU ANYMORE

OPEN 3 GATES TO SHARPEN YOUR FOCUS

K. LEE

Copyright © 2025 K. Lee

Published by Krystal Lee Enterprises LLC (KLE Publishing)
All rights reserved. No parts of this book may be reproduced, distributed, or used in any manner, including photocopying, recording, or other electronic or mechanical methods without the prior written permission of the copywriter owner, except for the use of brief quotations in a book review and certain noncommercial uses permitted by copyright law.

ISBN: 978-1-945066-66-5

Paperback:
All rights reserved. Please send comments and questions:
Krystal Lee Enterprises
Email: sales@KLEPub.com
Contact: Phone: 770-240-0089

To Reach the Author:
Email: me@authorklee.com or me@drkrystallee.com

Web: Authorkleecom
Social: IG, FB, Twitter, TikTok, Youtube
@AuthorKLee

Printed in the United States of America.

Disclaimer

The information in this book was correct at the time of publication, but the Author does not assume any liability for loss or damage caused by errors or omissions. These are my memories, from my perspective, and I have tried to represent events as faithfully as

possible.

Acknowledgments

I extend my gratitude to everyone who has supported me during my development. It's with that same heart that I present this second book in the Embrace Your Crown Series to you.

Thank you to my children, family, and Royals with the Embrace Your Crown First Sunday's Meetup Group!

To my incredible Father God (Yah) and my Savior Yashua the Christ, thank you for entrusting me with this powerful series to impact lives.

Shalom (Peace and blessings) to every reader.

Table of Contents

Dedication	7
Introduction	11
Seek First	17
Where's Your Beginning	35
What Do you Believe	53
Adjust Your Focus	69
Remember What You Did Before	95
Put It All On the Table	121
Transform Go Beyond Change	151
About the Author	157
Resources	159

DEDICATION

Why this series is for you…

I dedicate this series to the ladies and men who know they need a fresh perspective on life to make changes in their lives. This series, Embrace Your Crown, was written to empower you and help bring a guiding light to a task that could be daunting…finding you. Finding your purpose for living, why you are here on earth, and knowing where to go from here is at the core of this series's message.

I know it looks hard, it is uncomfortable, and the burden on your heart can be heavy. My intent is to share what has made my life lighter. What has helped me know that I was born for a reason and a purpose. What has shown me what I cannot do on my own and how it can be done with God. We can achieve great works and experience breakthroughs

Dedication - Embrace Your Crown

with power and wise counsel. In the safety of wise counsel, dreams are established (Proverbs 15:22). What is impossible for man is made possible with the power of the Living Word.

We don't live off of bread, the food we eat, and the houses we sleep in don't provide the shelter that some of us need. We need to drink from a living well. We need to eat food that is nutrient-rich so we are not hungry as we leave. We need substance. We need power and to focus our effort on what will work so we don't burn out from what has not worked.

We need rest from the toiling without reason, success, and limited power. We need to rebuild our confidence and learn that we are here at this point in life because there is more. I want to remind you that there is still more for you. There is more, no matter your age, past, history, or story. If you are here breathing, there is an assignment for you!

With great anticipation, I dedicate this book to those who would dare to find their place in the world at this time. It is too easy to say and live beneath our purpose for living. It is too easy to be absorbed in our thoughts, feelings, and emotions. This is not to say that this isn't a lot because it can be, but it is important to press through the pain to be free!

Wow, what a marvel. If you can get a glimpse of freedom for a moment, this book series will help remind you of what the goal of life through the midst of challenges points to. This book will help you sharpen that focus to sustain you during the tests and trials and remind you how to stay light as a feather as you carry heavy loads.

Yes, it is work, but not like you think. You can cast a mountain into the sea, but how can you lift it or how does it move? Focus on what freedom is, what you desire, and what you are called to become, and allow that to overshadow anything that would rise up against it. Condemn everything that would rise up in your heart or mind to battle the Word of truth concerning you to try and convince you you can't and be transformed to know that you can. Determine in your heart that you will.

Of course, I give thanks to my Master, Savior, Redeemer, Healer, and Author and Finisher of my Faith. Thank you for giving me a word to share with those who need You more. Who needs you to change every aspect of their lives. You are all-powerful, and there is nothing too hard for You. You are loving and kind, and with You, we can live and endure every burden with a light heart and mind.

It is with the heart You gave me that I am able to refocus my heart and keep it stayed on You as heavy and unsuspected events take my life by storm. For those going through tender moments, we will focus our hearts on becoming lighter—Shalom to you

Dedication - Embrace Your Crown

and your family, always from my heart to yours.

If you want to connect with me please take a moment to add me to your phone. You can also connect with me online to follow me on social pages like IG, FB, X, LinkedIn, Youtube, and More. Scan the QR and fill out the quick form to connect and receive bonus offers from the Embrace Your Crown Series.

Lastly, I have a free gift for you Royals. Yes, I call you royalty. You are a Queen: Qualified, Unique, Ethical, Encouraging, and Natural. King: Keen, Integrity, Natural, Generous. Access the series monthly public group: First Sundays EYC, get additional resources on books and content, or join a mentor program associated with one of the books with the QR below.

INTRODUCTION

CONNECTING THE DOTS

"I can do all things through him who strengthens me."
Philippians 4:13

When I first heard this series drop into my heart, it was not built on having a three-part series. It started as one book, Embrace Your Crown: Open 7 Gates to Find and Overcome Heartbreak. When I got the title, I was nervous to write the book and I even thought of canceling the writing process.

When you are doing the real work as you write, no AI, but you and the pages, the content, the feelings, the passion, the intent, it can be overwhelming. The emotions you feel as you share your life, heart, and passion in pages can overtake you in a good sense. It can move you to tears and push you to

Introduction - Embrace Your Crown

rethink your decisions.

As I started to write this book, I questioned if I wanted to be this open in my books. I asked myself, is this too much? Have you ever felt that you were giving too much? More than necessary and far above what you felt was comfortable for you? I felt that way as I started writing the first book.

I am a firm believer in not writing books for exploitation's sake. I would rather not write or share if what I am sharing or asking of someone else is too much! I don't believe you have to share your guts in the pages, but you want to ensure you leave the book feeling as if your purpose was fulfilled. You completed what you set out to do.

I had to look again for why I started this series and be intentional about how I wanted it to be received. This led to the start of the first book. I started writing this book because I had emotional pains for where the scares impacted me in other phases of my life. I didn't know the full extent of this pain and questioned if my story and journey could impact others.

I wondered for a bit if my stories were relevant or could help. It was at that moment, when I was in chapter seven roughly, that I witnessed my daughter living out my same mistakes growing up. It is admirable to take on the pains of others, but it is wrong to allow others to be misused to protect the guilty.

My daughter witnessed a guy stealing a book from an event we were attending, and at that moment, I asked her, "Why did you allow him to take it and not tell any of us when you saw it?" She replied, "I didn't want to be disrespectful." It was at that moment I realized that if I didn't write this book, many girls or women, boys or men, would think to protect the abuser over the victim. They could assume that speaking up is disrespectful.

When the moment mattered, they would be silent. When someone said or did something, they would be loyal to the wrong person. I had to tell her that day she was not being disrespectful, and she should have spoken up not only then but always. I knew I had to speak up and couldn't bite my tongue in this book.

SCAN THE QR TO

ORDER: BLESS THE WORKS OF MY HANDS

As I finished the first book, I realized I had more to learn and share. I revealed the seven gates to heartbreak but wanted to share more about unbelief. When we discover where our heartbreak is and

Introduction - Embrace Your Crown

start to do the work, we also have to look at what we believe about ourselves now. Your beliefs don't change as quickly as we may want them to. We might need to rethink everything we have been told, felt, or perceived about the world around us.

I knew this wasn't a chapter, but I needed a book to dedicate to the subject matter. I knew that several gates belonged to the topic, and I had to first identify the steps in my journey. After reflection, the gates were revealed to be five. If you feel that you are not currently battling the trauma of your past, you might be struggling to believe for greater than what you have already had.

You might feel that the pain, the problems, or the life you are living is the bed you made, and you have to live in it. However, what if the field was rigged against you? What if you no longer believe what you believed before? What if you realized what you believed before wasn't you at all?

Embrace Your Crown is this series' name because we must embrace who we are to know why we are here. If you have ever felt inadequate, you must ask why. Why do I feel this way? What am I called to achieve that supports this internal dialogue? How can I turn the table because this feeling is heavy on me, and I need something different?

When you are a mother of a two-year-old,

they need something different from you. When your children are twelve, it is different again. When they are twenty-two or thirty-two, it is different yet again. What you will find, however, is that in every phase, they need you. How they need you changes, as does your purpose in life. What the change really is is growth.

As we grow, the vision that was in part to begin with starts to be revealed more and more. You go from knowing a little to learning more and more. You go from seeing a little to a bigger part of the picture. As you start seeing further, you can appreciate where you have come from. It can encourage you to believe there is more still to come.

If the past has been filled with pain, it can be hard to believe anything different than what you have experienced. Yet, it can be different. That is the power of overcoming what you believe and exchanging that for what He, God, has said concerning your future. The younger you are, the longer you get to rest in His wonderful splendor on earth. As we get older, He can redeem your time, certainly.

We need to focus on what He plans for us and not what our past, our pain, or with our limited beliefs might have us believe. It all begins with knowing a fundamental truth and allowing it to be your faith's foundation! The foundation for how you live, move, why you breathe, and can have hope for any-

Introduction - Embrace Your Crown

thing. The truth, what you must focus on, is that you are equipped to live the life Yah has for you.

You were born with a purpose, on purpose, for a purpose! So what is the purpose? Why now? Are you determined to keep your focus on the actual mission and separate yourself from the lies and distractions surrounding you? I want you to close your eyes as you hear this read to you again: You were born with a purpose, on purpose, for a purpose!

SCAN THE QR TO

ORDER: BLESS THE WORKS OF MY HANDS

There are no mistakes, and you are here not by accident but for a purpose. The focus for this book that concludes this series is Embrace Your Crown: Open 3 Gates to Sharpen Your Focus. How do you bring your life into focus? You do that by "Seeking first the Kingdom of God and His righteousness, and all things will be added to you!"

Let's explore this final book that will bring the series together and help cement a way forward to make your way easy and your burden light.

SEEK FIRST

The Kingdom of God

"But seek first the kingdom of God and his righteousness, and all these things will be added to you." Matthew 6:33

So what's the Kingdom of God, anyway? Relax, this isn't a chapter committed to sending you to church. I want to explain to you the foundation of the basics of life so that you know on what facts you have established your foundation. It's simple: you cannot have a plan for going forward if you are stuck on something irrelevant or not applicable to you.

When we were birthed on this earth, we had a purpose. Yes, we still have a purpose and a choice for how we will participate in why you were created. We don't get to argue with the reason nor define it in the sense you didn't control your existence but someone Greater than you.

Parents are trying, and so is science, to create the perfect child the parents want. Yet, ensuring your child is born with green eyes, a type of hair, color, skin tone, etc., doesn't make sense in the grand scheme of things. You are saying, in short, that you know better than the Creator Himself for what you need. Ironically, many of these same people don't know how to fix their lives based on the choices they have made of their own choosing.

What makes us all-knowing about what kind of child we need or who needs us? Are there perfect people in the world? No. Are there parents that should not have been parents? Some can argue, yes. But, what makes us not see that every soul, no matter their look, intellect, financial picture, or other features, Yah can use them to create the world He designed.

Do you know if this were all a game rigged by God to see what people would do if they had free will, and He already knew your life's course, He would be justified? It might sound unfair. It might sound unjust to have a God that would allow all this to be created to have only one way to enter the Kingdom of God, right?

But what exactly is the Kingdom of God, and why is it important that you be there? Many of us were told about the church. We were told about going to church and being good Christians. We were indoctrinated with ideas, concepts, and ways of thinking that could be argued were passed down from those who used the same knowledge to enslave the world.

Many who distance themselves from the church are not so much distancing themselves from Yah, but the ideologies they see have problems. What if the churches you have seen, only two of them actually please God? In the Bible, it speaks about existing churches and the problems that God has with each of them. Yes, a church can be in error, and many of them are, if not most, unfortunately.

So what do we do? Do we throw the baby out with the bath water? Do we chuck understanding of the Kingdom of God because we don't want to attend a church full of satanists, witches, backbiters, liars, thieves, and the rest? Do we say that God doesn't exist because when you experienced the church or those claiming to represent it, they did not leave a good impression in your heart?

What did they say or do that has you questioning going to church? A better question: what has the church done that the Bible would record how there was only one church that Yah approved out of the seven? Yashua, Jesus the Christ, in a vision, showed a vision to John. A vision, in this case, is a dream that is kind of like how you can dream while awake.

He saw the Messiah, the first born-again human, come to him and say fear not. How many of us would have jumped out of our skin if we thought we saw a ghost? I have seen countless videos and can attest to what fear can have people do to themselves. When we are afraid, some of us want to fight. We are bold enough to start swinging our fists, not knowing if we will hit a thing.

Others are ready to run. It can be pitch black, and you cannot see two feet in front of you. You will take off praying not to run into something. We can feel trapped in an enclosed space and see something jump out of a box or run towards us and faint quicker than our hearts can catch up with what we saw. Fear can have us do strange things, can't it?

Yes, some of these pranks are not real. So what about your dreams? What about the nightmares you have that keep you up at night? What about those who worry about their greatest fears coming true? What about those who saw a loved one die, get hurt, or get injured in a dream? Have you ever been chased or felt a strong sense of darkness come over your body and hold you down or make you feel like you were going to die?

We all have had one or many of these experiences that could point to something we find hard to explain and sometimes remember to share when we wake up. What we are left with oftentimes is the impact of the dream. We can feel scared, hurt, powerless, ashamed, or lost. We don't always know what to do with the dream or even what they mean, so we either ignore it, pray about it, or bury it, hoping it doesn't happen.

Have you ever seen something in your dreams manifest in your reality or in the lives of those you love? I have a lot of dreams. When I wake up, the first thing I do is pray about what they mean, especially if I got instructions. I have seen many of my dreams come to pass for myself and others, and I have learned to pray dreams in, rebuke what I saw, or pray for comfort if the event is unavoidable, etc.

All of this proves something, however. There is a realm called a dream realm that touches our natural lives. There are things we can dream, see, or experience that we cannot explain, but we know how it made us feel and how it manifested. This becomes the evidence that proves there are spiritual powers that exist outside ourselves. There are entities that speak to you while you sleep or dream awake. Some thoughts come to you that are not your words but are a conversation you are having with someone–but who?

In the dream that John was having, who he saw introduced Himself by given His name, and also explained the dream that John had. If I see a man with white hair like wool, likely long because he was a Nazarene, and they don't cut their hair like Samson, who had seven locs. His eyes were intent like fire, and He said He had the keys to Death and Hades. His eyes tell you where He has been and establishes His power.

When we see demons, many of us are out! If they are fake or real, we don't stick around if they strike fear in us. Not only did the Messiah enter hell, but came out with the keys to control hell and death. Then it says his feet were like bronze. Bronze is a brown, golden color made of a metal that symbolizes strength and stability. Bronze is often used to create mechanisms that require strength, like bearings, springs, and bushings.

It puts a new perspective on gathering my

bearings, right? So, John sees Him, an Yashua/Jesus explains the vision John saw. He tells him the seven stars are the seven angels over the church. And the seven lampstands are the seven churches. John's instructions were simple: to deliver the letters or information to the churches.

Why am I sharing this information? Before we say we don't like church, we first have to know what church is. Before we say we don't want to be in the Kingdom of God, we need to know what it is like. We all have a version of heaven in our hearts and minds, and that's cool. But what is life supposed to be like before that eventful day?

Give me just a little longer, and I will explain quickly. To the first church, Ephesus (Revelation 2:1), he said this church was great at keeping people in line. They had a sharp eye to point out non-believers in leadership. They were good at testing people to see if they were genuine, but they had a flaw. The Messiah said they were a loveless church.

Have you ever gone to a church and didn't feel love? You felt judgment, a prying eye, and unbearable discipline. You felt pressure as soon as you hit the door and wondered if the church would accept you, a sinner who knows they are not right. So, feeling condemnation and not love, you didn't return.

The next church is Smyrna (Revelation 2:8). He told them that persecution was coming. Unrighteous outcomes will befall them not because God is displeased with them but because tribulation is also a choice of man's free will. These believers will be thrown in jail.

Some were forced to renounce what they believed or were robbed of their things–even killed. These people who torment believers and persecute the church claim to be Jews, but they are the synagog of satan (Revelation 3:9).

These people claim to be good-natured and doing God a favor. They claim to work for humanity or the good but are liars. They are out for blood and to crush the good in the Church for their gain. They are silencing your posts, kicking you out of leadership roles, and making you feel like hell is hovering above your finances, job, career, health, and wealth. But you are rich, although the world will tell you you are poor. But how many feel like going to church doesn't seem like a blessing but pain? Would you want to go to this church?

How many would be tempted to be like the third church, Pergamos (Revelation 2:12), the compromising church? This church was good at preaching the Word of God and knowing the power of it. They were good-looking on the outside, but when you enter the church, you can see that satan has a throne room there. Within churches that practice Balaam worship or the ideals of the Nicolations that Yah hates, you find compromise (Revelation 2:15).

People who are willing to bend the rules to obtain wealth or explore sexual sin. These people are selfish and self-seeking. They will use the Word of God or the church to promote their own agenda, not the Kingdom of God. They are sleeping with people who need healing and lying about their actions in the church. The church has a good word, but they have compromised fruit.

Then you have the fourth church, Thyatira (Revelation 2:18). Thyatira was the church that didn't hide any of its ways. They were openly corrupt and followed after Jezebel, a witch who lies and says she is a prophetess of Yah. This woman preached and taught doctrines that encouraged sexual immorality. This church will teach that sexual deviance according to God is permissible. The Messiah warned that Yah would give her time to repent, but if she didn't and those who practice her teachings, the would be sent to a sickbed (Revelation 2:22).

The people who she has trained will come to nothing and will die. This could mean mortal death, having no ministry, or being cut off from the Father completely. He said that this would be done so that others would see it and know that what was spoken by Yashua was fact. Good thing you dodge the judgment of this church, right?

Church number five is the dead church (Revelation 3:1). Sardis is the church that received the letter to say although they claim that they are alive, they are dead. They are a church with a form of godliness but no power (2 Timothy 3:5). This church has a few things going right, but they need more to please Yah. What they are given is not in line with the Kingdom of God, but their ideals, antics, or events are more worldly than spiritual.

This church struggles to keep people coming;

whenever they think they are going up, they drift back down. These churches have dry messages, old recycled messages that they preach from when they were on fire for God. The church is as dry as a tumbleweed; many know it, although some feel obligated to stay.

Philadelphia, the faithful church, had by far the best letter requiring no repentance (Revelation 3:7). Their letter revealed that this church is under an open heaven. This church is promised preservation and protection. This church, although it suffered under the hands of fake Jews, will not be overtaken. In fact, this church will see those who thought to crush them come and worship in their buildings.

This church will see a marvel in that those who sought their destruction will return to ask for their help. Those who did not like you but tried every way to hurt you or the church you are in, the Father will send resources to come and assist you even when you have little strength left. If members leave, if people don't like the messages, if you're blasted on the news for being this or that, holding on by a string, He will send the help to rescue you on time because even under immense pressure, you did not fold.

The last church to receive a letter was Laodiceans (Revelation 3:14). This church was described as lukewarm, not good for nothing the Father has in mind. This church claims they are doing well, have no problems, the world is roses outside, and paint a superficial version of Jesus. This is the version that pictures him not as a redeemer and one who sets the captives free but as the ones who bring humanity options to be happy.

He said this church doesn't realize they are wretched, miserable, blind, and naked. This church has good works but doesn't know the power of God. They think their achievements are a reflection of a good relationship with Him, but it is the absence of Him instead. This church houses the people who say they got it together and have no problems, but when they go home, all hell is breaking loose, and those who can see in the spirit or know your business know it.

What is common for all six churches that had issues was the call to come to repentance. Repentance means acknowledging that how you have been living your life is wrong and not in order. It means that you realize there is more to life, to what you have and know, than you have settled for.

Yes, you can have achievements. Yes, you can be wealthy or poor. Yes, you can look good on paper but be a living fool on the inside. You can be bankrupt of the Divine, and as you live, more hell will circle about you than love.

The absence of love is evidence that you need more of Yah in your life. You need more Word. You need to be around people who can show you the divine church and reveal the Kingdom of God. I have said all this to get to a rather simple concept: What is the Kingdom of God?

Many think the Kingdom of God is a church building. It is not. It is a connection of people who are aligned with the Truth of God and committed to living the principles of God on earth so that those who watch you will see His Kingdom on earth. We know the prayer, "Thy kingdom come, Your will will be done, on earth as it is in heaven" (Matthew 6:10).

We are to bring the Kingdom of Heaven on earth! We are to be a living example of heaven and increase the Good Lord's footprint right here where we live. We are not to pretend that we have nothing God has helped us with although we know He exists. No, for many of us, he pulled us out of hell!

He pulled us out of relationships and toxic situations. He deals with messy people, and none of us smelled like roses when He met us. Some of us have lost our way for various reasons. Some of us are tired and want out. Some of us see success and then see drought. We are on a seesaw that is now making us sick.

SCAN THE QR TO

ORDER: "LOOK FOR THE DRIP AND EXPECT THE OUTPOUR"

We want progress and the things that sum up the abundant life, but do we want to be part of the Kingdom of God? Do you want to be a agent of change on earth? Do you want to be a person who brings the good news to men, women, and children? Do you want to be a reflection of the Kingdom of Heaven on earth?

Are you part of the Body of Christ? Are you willing to use your gifts, talents, and ideas to bless the Kingdom of God, or are you more concerned with building up your own wealth by any means necessary? Are you okay with living holy until it costs you something, or are you willing to give it all back to the One who gave it to you?

When we seek first the Kingdom of God and His righteousness, all things will be added to us (Matthew 6:33). What does the Father promise you exactly? Does He promise you success? Good health? Marriage? Or a simple one, a happy life?

He promises a purpose-filled life with direction, support, and power. We think power equals never having a bad day. It makes sense, but to know you have power, you have to encounter problems that require it.

To know you are in good health, you may need to see sickness. You may need a off day so you don't take for granted being well. On the cross, Yashua bore all sickness and experienced the pain. Why should He have to learn it if He never sinned to receive the punishment? Sin leads to death is the word (James 1:15). So why should He have died if He had all power and He didn't deserve it? He was a living vessel that brought honor to God.

Because He was used to set those free who thought that God could not save a wretch like them, He had to experience hell and even go there to deliver us from ourselves. He needed to show us the power of obedience, even unto the grave. He wouldn't ask something of you that He didn't do. So, He suffered it all so that when He says all things He can do, you cannot question His word.

Now, when we seek first the Kingdom of God, we are seeking to live out our purpose and fulfill the reason we were put on earth, no matter the circumstances, with righteousness and a pure heart given to us through salvation. Yashua, Jesus was the first born-again man, we are now to be the next. We are to be born again so that we can be of the same mind and follow in the same footsteps, although we are not perfect, we are made perfect in Christ (Hebrews 10:12, 14).

If you have been serving, working, helping, or living a life that is honorable or not, this book is going to help you lock in and focus on how you can be part of the Kingdom of God. How you can live heaven on earth and be an example of Yah's goodness. How you can be made light and encouraged to endure all things, because you can see clearly now your purpose.

If you were tired, here is your new wind. If you were going to quit, hold on. If you thought you weren't good enough, that's okay; there is one who is, and Jesus/Yashua said He will pay your debts. I got you! If you have problems you cannot solve, the whole earth is the Lord's. If you think you are too far away and He cannot redeem you or save you from your mess. He told us already He went into hell and set captives free(Ephesians 4:8). What should you be afraid of?

Death? He has those keys, too! Nothing is too hard for Him and those called according to His purpose. Let's Embrace Our Crown and Open 3 Gates to Sharpen our Focus!

Thinking Points!

A. What are your thoughts about the churches you have visited?
B. If your life represented a church, what church would you be closest aligned to?
C. Have you determined to make the righteousness of God the compass for leading your life?
D. What does seeking the will of God look like for you?
E. What areas of your life currently are you not seeking the advice of scripture to guide your decision making?

Now, I want you to do the Self Check-In to *Embrace Your Crown*!

I. Let's Check You In!
   A. Situation
      1. Are you convinced that living life your way hasn't given you the fulfillment you need in life?
   B. Change
      1. To welcome the change you

want in your life, are you willing to seek first the Kingdom of God and what the Word says about your behavior and actions?

C. Endurance

1. Following Yah doesn't mean you won't have to go through anything. Sometimes it will be unjust and unfair, are you willing to see how even that can work to your good through Christ?

D. Persevere

1. When we have been patient, we might think our suffering should end. That we should get the house we want because of how hard we worked for it. I tell you, that what the Father says you will have, you shall have it. Though it tarries, wait for it keeping your focus on the fulfillment of His Word.

E. Acknowledgments

1. No one can say they have lived a life perfectly pleasing or perfectly aligned to the Will of God. We need the help of His Holy Spirit and the Word to make us perfect. We are not and will never be perfect in and of ourselves.

F. Re-Purpose
1. If you were struggling with church hurt that has shut you out of a relationship with Yah, understand that not every church who preaches sermons from the Bible is a Godly pleasing church. There are many types of churches, but only two pleased God. People are not perfect, so we all need grace and so does the church.

G. Help?
1. If an aspect of this chapter was difficult and you want to talk about where you are, please do. Be encouraged; you are not alone. We have free and paid resources to help you work through this series. Skilled coaches, therapists, and speakers are here to help.

Sometimes, we get stuck in a process or want to discover more about what makes us or has made us who we are. Do not feel like you can't linger on a thinking point, question, or chapter. If you need help throughout this book at any point, I want you to contact me and my team. We are a network of coaches, counselors, and prayer warriors ready to help you Embrace Your Crown, connect the dots, and go from where you are to where you are born to go.

H.	*Embrace Your Crown* Affirmations: Let's make some declarations!
1.	I will not let church hurt scare me away from building a relationship with God.
2.	I am not perfect, but will be made perfect through Christ who strengthens me.
3.	I am not alone because God sent His Son to show me the way.
4.	I will not seek first my desires but the Kingdom of God and His righteousness.
5.	It is the plans of God that will see is the final say on matters of my heart and life's direction.
6.	In my weakness, I am made strong through Christ who strengthens me!
7.	I will not water down the power of Yah by compromising the Word.
8.	I will stand on the truth of God

and find a family of believers that is pursuing holiness.
9. I am ready to *Embrace My Crown*! Embracing who I am and who I was born to become!
10. I am ready to TRANSFORM and Go BEYOND Change!

Defining Your Roots

" Let your eyes look directly forward, and your gaze be straight before you." Proverbs 4:25

If you are breathing, congratulations, you were born on purpose, and you can still pursue it. When we are formed in our mother's belly, there is a plan at work, and your natural gifts point to the development of your purpose. Your natural gifts are what you need to pursue your purpose and point you to your true north.

So, if your talents, abilities, and gifts are lighting the way to why you are here on earth, what have they been saying to you? Yes, you can have a job that may feel loosely connected to your gifts. You can use your gifts or talents to live life, but that doesn't mean that's all you have to give.

Where's Your Beginning - Embrace Your Crown

I know growing up, I had several natural talents that I use everyday still. Some talents I had to learn how to use them better. I had to become more innovative with my approach to integrating some gifts into my everyday life, like with production. When I was born to my comical family, we were all gifted speakers, comedians, and people who love people.

Even for my oldest brother, who says he is not a people person, I cannot name someone who has met him and didn't feel at home. He is an easy person to talk to. My mom is easy; my oldest sister and my baby brother all know no stranger. The only one that might put you on your toes if you are acting up is my baby sister. However, she also works in an environment where she engages people on a regular basis, and her clients love her.

So, this would be a clear example of how my family has been gifted with being relatable, caring for others, and having a heart to connect. In my case, I certainly don't know a stranger, and learning to use technology has expanded my heart to reach across country lines, cultures, and age groups.

How we use our talent is very different. My mom uses her talent in the life insurance industry. She enjoys helping people to cover their family members throughout life and especially for burial. She has seen what not having burial insurance does to a family and the burden it causes. Having a GoFundMe to sponsor funerals gets old, and if you can have an investment account that can help children have thousands of dollars by the time they are forty, how

much could that change a community?
	She has found part of her calling in life in insurance, but she is always ready to give you a sermon or bible study based on what she is reading and feels compelled to share. My sister has a nail salon, and she helps people enjoy the simple things. She has always been meticulous when we were children, picking at her skin, something like that. I don't know how she got so focused in this industry, but it doesn't surprise me how good she is at nail art and design.

	She went to school and is a certified nail tech. I am proud of her because she puts her money where her mouth is and dares to dream big and then bigger than that. She is still talking about school even now. My head swells at how much school she is willing to take to pursue her interest in both the esthetician and medical fields.

	My older brother is into fashion, but he has always been a hard worker, keeping two jobs. He likes fine things, boogie living as we call it, but he works to enjoy it. He creates limited pieces mostly in his spare time, but someday, I am sure he will push to make more time to do what he loves. Life is always changing, and he does a great job of keeping a fresh perspective on what inspires him.

	I admire that he knows how to be patient and doesn't beat himself up because he is not where some of his friends have progressed to. He loves his gift, but I would say fashion is a dream that is still in the making. I like that he has the heart to make specialty shoes for people with webbed feet or unevenness. Growing up with the problem made him sensitive to others who struggled to find fashionable and comfortable footwear.

He is a walking miracle, for sure. The doctors told him he wouldn't walk, and if he did, he would struggle. My mom got him braces, and with prayer, that changed. He walks fine, and the corrective measures they took when he was young paid off big; our family is forever grateful.

My older sister is so talented with conflict resolution so it doesn't surprise me that she is a store manager for a large store chain. She has been consistent since she started. She is a go-getter but a woman who will not stop no matter what. When her heart and mind agree, she is unstoppable.

I love that she uses her personality to help people find their purpose in the simple things that might be temporary or long-term. Some people see department stores as a stop before they do what they love. It is warming when you can meet a manager who generally cares for you and wants to help you be great for wherever you go.

She is good company, and so is my baby brother. He is a truck driver who found his passion later in life. He got a 98%, taking the test for the first time. He always said he wanted to go back to school, but none of us knew what school he would pick. My baby brother has been a free spirit and perhaps getting away with a lot because of his age and birth order. Now, my mom has no children younger than their 30s, so we are excited that he has found something he wants to stick with.

K. Lee

He is a long-haul driver, so he usually drives in pairs cross country a few days out of the week. It works because he likes to tell jokes, be around people, and stay away from pollen and other allergens. He is a severe asthmatic, and finding a position to fit his needs and interests was a bit tricky. Seeing him send us laugh pics and share his excursion stories has been great.

So what about you? What is a gift within you or about your family that has rubbed off? How have you brought out your unique skills for the world to benefit? Finding our place can be something we know immediately or take years to develop. For me, I knew since I was young what I would love to do.

I have always had a heart to tell stories. When I was younger, I would sing songs that had a story. Re-enact movies and other skits I came up with to make people laugh. I enjoyed performing, so I would join dance competitions where I won more times than I lost. Although I love entertaining, what I like most is writing.

In school, I learned to embrace telling stories but more so being able to express my thoughts in writing. I was the talker in my family. If you ask any of my siblings, they will tell you, "Krystal was the talker." I got flack when I was younger, and being older, I can empathize. Sometimes, I just have a moment of silence, but my eldest son, who everyone says is my personality twin, keeps on talking.

I get it now. Why my mom at times, could come off as agitated or overwhelmed. I can say that, being older, I have learned to fall back a lot and not share as much as I could, sometimes a little goes a long way, right? When we are learning our gifts it can be a humbling time. We can want to be ourselves, which is too much for others.

When we are too much for those around us, it doesn't feel warm and fuzzy inside. It can make you feel rejected, embarrassed, and prompt you to look for the nearest exit. I had several uncomfortable moments as I learned what a healthy balance was for me. Time is something we cannot rush, and a process that doesn't make apologies for taking as long as it does.

We can want to grow up overnight, but it still won't happen. No matter how mature you become, you still have to deal with the hiccups of time. I learned early on that it didn't bother me too much for how fast or slow time occurred as long as I felt like I was making progress toward my goals. If you are feeling a bit in a funk right now, I want you to focus on how you are spending your time right now.

I want you to embrace a quality my older brother has to relax and enjoy the moment. Yes, time isn't promised, and we don't know how long we have, but that shouldn't scare us but make us want to live even better. We should grow more committed to our growth process as we experience life. There is always something to do under the sun, and the longer you live, the more you can experience.

I used to feel that I had to do the most as young as possible to ensure I left my children with a leg up. In black and brown communities, we may feel at a disadvantage and shoulder the responsibility to make up ground. I know I have felt the pressure to fulfill assignments financially, especially that I didn't know they could get done.

I needed to breathe. I remember when I was working every day of the week. I thought working ten-hour days, or however long Monday to Sunday, meant I would arrive and achieve more. Have you noticed that in our day and time, with all the medicine, advancements, and knowledge, we die younger than our ancestors?

It didn't take me long to be convinced that living a balanced life was far greater than burning my energy at all ends. I had to establish healthy boundaries like keeping the Sabbath, not working weekends, and cutting my brain off after writing or editing a chapter, even if it was for twenty minutes. When I would return back to work, I was refreshed and able to press through deadlines even faster.

Taking a break for me has made me a better worker, business owner, and mother. I used to care a lot about financially providing for my children and ensuring they had what they needed. I soon realized that working at all times to make money seemed great, but they didn't remember half of the things I bought them.

They wanted my time just as much as they wanted the things. Finding the balance of spending time and money was no easy quest. I had to master my schedule if I had hoped to balance my life. Children don't look at just what you tell them but also at what they see you do. How you live does matter.

We don't always know who is watching and taking notes from our lives. These eyes and followers you cultivate become your testimonials and validation of how well you have taught someone else. Our children are the first examples of our teaching and leadership. What we learn from our parents, we tend to share with the world willingly or begrudgingly.

You can control how you interact with how you were raised and what you choose to value and implement on a regular basis. But as we learn what we like, dislike, and discover our true values, don't be surprised if they are at our core in making these decisions. Parents are our first teachers. How they teach us, love us, or guide us is important for what becomes the standard in our lives.

For your life, what would you say are your wants or desires? What can you not live without? What do you define as good or good enough for you? Not all the answers to these questions you may like or may be good for you. I want you to try to be honest because this will help you understand how you are living now.

When we realize why we think the way we do or want what we want in life, it helps us to better understand ourselves and our upbringing. What I learned about my youth was that I hated to disappoint those I loved. I wanted my parents to be proud of me, and I would go above and beyond what was expected to avoid trouble, too.

K. Lee

I developed a habit of giving excuses for others or covering their errors to help things stay peaceful. I often would take a loss in conversation and be quiet when I really wanted to say more. Growing up with a mom who taught me to stay in a child's place and not speak if a question wasn't being asked told me to be silent even if I had the answer. I could see the obvious but would wait until I knew I had clearance to speak.

The last thing you wanted was to be backhanded because you said something at a time you weren't supposed to. In my era, reading the room was required if you wanted tv and not to be embarrassed. I would lock eyes with my mom before answering questions to know how honest I could be. Sometimes, we struggled and couldn't tell anyone about it.

It really did shape my mind to see life as a struggle my entire life. I didn't have an upbringing that brought stability, so someone providing for me was a gift I saw innumerable value. Likewise, I was used to working for everything I have ever gotten as it pertains to things like my phone, car, housing, etc since I turned sixteen and onward.

I got my first apartment myself at age 18, and I have lived on my own for the most part, except for temporary times of staying with family as I shuffled to my new place. I tried not to stay with anyone longer than a month or up to three. I know no matter how much someone loves you, you can wear out your welcome, and I wanted to leave before that happened.

That meant moving quickly. I could not expect others to treat them like how I do and have my rules. My children were all homeschooled for many years, so they grew accustomed to varied schedules that accommodated their personal needs. Life for us has been flexible, but school times and living with others don't always permit that to happen.

I can see the disappointment on their faces when the rules change, and that is not always a bad thing. However, I realized not everything I learned to desire from my childhood has set me up for the best outcome as an adult. I had to unlearn things and determine how they would benefit me. I was never a yeller and hated when people argued. In my adult life, I am not big on confrontation.

I try to find a peaceable road to resolve conflict, but sometimes that means everyone is not going to be happy. I have learned to accept that as I grew older. After bumping your head enough times and apologizing to everyone else but you, you learn to value yourself more. I am at that stage in my life now, but I had to understand how I got there. How I got to a point where I would marry, date, or consider a spouse that honestly didn't meet the needs I had.

Something I felt in my mind told me what I wanted was unrealistic. I believed I needed to settle for a good man, or a good enough man, instead of who I was looking for. I wouldn't say I was afraid of being alone or that I liked being around a spouse all the time. I honestly pick unavailable men who travel and are hardly around, so I can say I love my space. At the same time, I didn't require them to do much because I was so self-sufficient. The issue became when I might want to fall back and enjoy other aspects of life, and they felt I should run at the same pace they were.

I grew up with a single mother for the most part and so I learned to do for myself, but in my marriage, I didn't want that to be the case. Although I settled for scenarios that looked like a repeat of my upbringing, it would put a bitter taste in my mouth after a while. I wouldn't abandon them, of course, but I had to come to grips that this was something I did not like. It was a straw that was in the hat for our problems, but other issues ultimately would cancel the relationship.

I felt overly committed to people who I knew weren't as committed to me. At first, I tried to see past it, but after a while, my attention couldn't go anywhere else. Can you relate? I needed to learn how to get to this conclusion sooner than six years of dating or after a failed marriage. I had to train my wants and desires not to chase the things of comfort but my desire. Then, be content if I don't find it to be alone.

It took time to realize being single was better for me than being married. I am a firm believer in marriage, but for the man I believe needs to be in my life, and my setup hasn't been a match. I had someone tell me once my men picker was broken. Although they were partially joking, I heard the words, and I didn't want to make the same old mistakes any longer. I was content with spending the time to get to know myself and what I wanted or needed before jumping back out there.

Where's Your Beginning - Embrace Your Crown

I had to create an atmosphere that allowed me to think and reflect. Sometimes, we can be in a hostile, fast-paced environment that blocks our rational thinking. We could normally answer a question, but when we are in a high-stress situation, burdened or overwhelmed, our brain doesn't trigger the same.

They say never make a decision when you are hungry at the grocery store because you will take home everything. I try not to look for love when I am hurting or haven't considered my needs enough. When I am around people who are negative about something I desire, I find it harder to push past their voices to get what I want. If you want more than the people around you, you will have to change your circle.

This doesn't mean you eliminate people, but you need to limit their influence. As you limit the influence of people who are not going where you want to go, you will start to shape your lifestyle. Growing up, our lifestyle is likely a product of our parents and some of our choices. As we get older, our lifestyle can become the product of our choices.

I wanted to make sure every step I was making was helping me to Embrace My Crown and support my journey to becoming who I was born to be. When I saw the moments in my life that broke my heart and the responses I made, I saw how I got to my low areas in life. I started to realize why I avoided people or situations as an adult. I was able to even point to how my strengths developed.

Some of the choices we make in business

and as adults are an extension of our younger years. It isn't all bad but it likewise isn't all good. The first steps I had to take to understand my beginning started with embracing my story and seeing how I saw Time, Patience, Purpose, Patterns, Wants & desires, My Atmosphere, and Lifestyle.

I had to be brave and look at what might have negatively and positively influenced me. In my reflection, I realized heartbreak was a common thread for shaping how I responded later in life. The first book in this series, Embrace Your Crown: Open 7 Gates to Find and Overcome Heartbreak, had to be released. But it didn't stop there. I had to understand where to go from here, and that led me to the second book.

Yes, there is a lot to unpack about family, parenting, or our younger years and how we respond to heartbreak. I encourage you to read the first book to further unpack the seven gates if you haven't already. This series has a connection that allows you to drop in with any book, but they paint a full picture collectively.

SCAN THE QR TO

ORDER: "EMBRACE YOUR CROWN: OPEN 7 GATES TO FIND AND OVERCOME HEARTBREAK"

Thinking Points!

A. What were some of the good principles you learned as a child?

B. What were some negative tips you got from your parents by watching them or from something they told you?

C. What are the wants and desires you have for your life?

D. Are these desires yours, as a freely thinking adult, or are you still leaning on the influences of other's to define what you want or need to do?

E. Is there are area you need to take more control over to decide how you need to live to fulfill your purpose?

Now, I want you to do the Self Check-In to *Embrace Your Crown*!

I. Let's Check You In!
   A. Situation
      1. Have you found that there are some wants and desires you still are holding on to that are not good for your purpose?
   B. Change
      1. What actions do you feel you need to make to correct how

you think or why you think the way you do about a want or desire?

C. Endurance
1. Look at your progress and that of your family and see the beauty in your stories?

D. Persevere
1. No life will be perfect. Some of us get what we need early to have direction on how to move in life, while others will take more time. Be patient to know the day will come if you continue to seek it out and do the work to create an atmosphere to flourish in it.

E. Acknowledgments
1. There is a place and atmosphere where you will thrive. But wherever the Spirit of God is with you you can make it. Even if the cards are not aligned and you feel you are in the wrong state, things can change where you are to get you where you need to be. Pray for what you need to be in right position and not just for what you want to see yourself. You might not have the right direction, so praying the Father's will for your life will

refocus your life.

F. Re-Purpose

1. All roads don't lead to Rome, but any road can bring you to Christ Yashua/Jesus. There is nothing to difficult for him to change or impact in your life. Don't give up if you feel like life is all over the place. Keep reading and let's find where you are and work to bring love, healing, direction to impact your life for the better.

G. Help?

1. If an aspect of this chapter was difficult and you want to talk about where you are, please do. Be encouraged; you are not alone. We have free and paid resources to help you work through this series. Skilled coaches, therapists, and speakers are here to help.

Sometimes, we get stuck in a process or want to discover more about what makes us or has made us who we are. Do not feel like you can't linger on a thinking point, question, or chapter. If you need help throughout this book at any point, I want you to contact me and my team. We are a network of coaches, counselors, and prayer warriors ready to help you Embrace Your Crown, connect the dots, and go from where you are to where you are born to go.

H. *Embrace Your Crown* Affirmations: Let's make some declarations!
1. I will realign my wants and desires to be in the will of God.
2. I am not longer going to allow people who don't have what I need to influence me.
3. I will allow the foundation of my salvation, the Word of God to direct my path.
4. I will unlearn what I have learned that taught me toxic or unfruitful ways of dealing with life.
5. I am not too old to learn how to live a righteous life.
6. I trust that there is nothing too hard for Yah to change in my life.
7. The atmosphere I will keep will remain full of hope.
8. I will acknowledge and celebrate victories no matter how small

9.   by speaking up about them.
I will not beat myself up when I fail, but make a learning lesson for how to win.
10.   I am ready to *Embrace My Crown*! Embracing who I am and who I was born to become!
11.   I am ready to TRANSFORM and Go BEYOND Change!

WHAT DO YOU BELIEVE

Your Vision is the Distance

"Therefore we must pay much closer attention to what we have heard, lest we drift away from it." Hebrews 2:1

Doing the great work of discovering, finding, and committing to overcome heartbreak is brave. I know it sounds easy, but it is work and takes time. It took some of us a decade or longer to become who we are. It surely won't take reading a book one singular time for all that to be rewritten.

What has been established is that you are committed and intentional in changing your life. You are at a point in your life where you want to do some soul-searching to find you, your purpose, and what you believe. You are ready to establish your roadmap for life that extends beyond your parents and family history.

What Do You Believe - Embrace Your Crown

At this stage, you can jump out into the world. You can start looking at life with your own eyes and form your own decisions about how you feel. Understanding your patterns and the reason behind your habits will help you determine if they need to change. Have you heard about the family that made it a tradition to cut the turkey in half to cook it?

Essentially, three generations of women would cut the turkey in half instead of cooking the bird whole. When the fourth-generation child was coming up, she asked, why should we cut it in half and not just cook it whole? The mother said, "That is how Grandma taught me." The mother thought about her answer after she said it. She didn't tell her daughter, but she went to her mother and asked.

Her mother told her the same thing. But when a family member overheard the conversation, they said, "Your mom used to do that because her oven was too small to cook a full bird, so she began cutting it to fit." Not everything we were taught to do is necessary for today. Not all traditions carry the same level of importance. Sometimes, we keep doing the same things because it is easier to go with the flow than to question and wait around for answers.

When we don't spend the time to define why we do what we do, we can make our lives more difficult and not evolve. We have to determine what we believe and then move on that information to better the lives of others. When we lack belief or direction, it plays into what we will expect from the future and of ourselves.

If we have a worker's mentality, we can keep our heads down and not pay attention to anything outside the box. This might be good for remaining content with working a 9 to 5 or avoiding management, but it will not help you as an owner. A business owner needs to ask questions and get the most honest feedback. Business owners have to be solution-driven, which requires knowing the answers to tough questions.

If most people are content with doing what is easy or cheap, if you want to disrupt that pattern, you need to know how you are going to do that. If you were born into a family with limited means, in poverty, you would have to make changes not to repeat the familiar. If you want to have a healthy relationship with your children, and that wasn't present with your parents, you will have to be open to learning new things.

If you have been doing everything yourself with no help, but you don't have the results you need in life. If you feel lower instead of elevated or life has become more challenging than easy, you need to redefine what you believe and expand your belief. For book two, Embrace Your Crown: Open 5 Gates to Overcome Unbelief, we unpacked our belief system.

When we feel we have a huge uphill climb or lots of work to do, we can lean on wanting magic. We have all seen the movies where the character whips out their wand and twirls it to clean up their mess, and boom; all things are put right. In life, wouldn't we all like to avoid having to do the work to clean up our mess?

What Do You Believe - Embrace Your Crown

To be able to overlook the problems that might have been our fault or to pretend everything is fine when it is not isn't good. Contrary to popular belief, the best and fastest way to change your life is not by wishing it to change. You will, in fact, get nothing accomplished by laying on a blanket and staring up from the ground to the stars. If you are waiting on a shooting star to change your life, you are only shooting progress in the foot and delaying the changes that come without magic.

True life change takes work and something else that is not magic. It takes something that can look similar to magic: power. Moses in the Bible had power, but the magicians who tried to discredit what he was doing had magic. If you recall, when his staff was turned into a snake, the magicians did the same thing, only their snakes were eaten up by his.

Power is stronger than magic. Power is consistent, like electricity. It is a constant supply of energy that can provide what you need to get things done. Magic is like having a portable battery charging in your pocket. It works when you are in a pinch, but it will require power to get it back up again. It requires your pain to keep it fueled.

Magic uses dark matter, feelings, emotions, and ultimately, pain. Power is filled with the light; it requires belief, trust, and hope. Did you know that light can always cast out darkness? The light shines brighter than darkness, but the way this power makes you feel is the divine purpose of power. You were not meant to use your will to yield hell on earth but to be a beacon of hope and love.

SCAN THE QR TO

ORDER: "EMBRACE YOUR CROWN: OPEN 5 GATES TO OVERCOME UNBELIEF"

But it is hard to give something you don't have. We can all agree that love is what the world needs more of. Families need it, governments, political officials, and so forth. If we only knew and understood that God is Love, it would help us to believe for more than what we have.

The goodness of Yah, God, is that He has given us promises. These promises could be totally subject to our actions, but by mercy, they are not. While we were sinners and wanted nothing to do with God, He gave His Son the Word to be a bridge to connect us back to Him. Connecting us back to truth, love, honesty, virtue, holiness, and every good work.

It is not the will of Yah for us to be broken, busted, disrespected, abused, or misused. He gave us a promise that vengeance is His and He will fight our battles with us (Romans 12:19). He will never leave you nor forsake you is what He promised (Deuteronomy 31:8). If you have the confidence that God is with you, how can you not have the power to achieve great things?

In the Presence of Yah, mysteries, miracles, signs, and wonders take place (Mark 16:17-18). We have to make room for a miracle because they don't just happen on their own. Our obedience working by faith opens the door for miracles to come. If we are doing right and something we didn't ask for comes, I would argue that isn't mercy but a miracle. When we get something we didn't ask for but need when we are undeserving, I would say that is mercy.

Many people say they need a miracle. There are songs about it. Christmas movies that talk about it. Have you ever wondered what the biggest difference is between wishing on a star, being lucky, or having a miracle?

Wishing is having a strong desire for something but having no clear direction for attaining it. It is something we do as humans when we want something, but in my opinion, don't believe it will come to pass. It's a long shot that we need more faith to pray for and believe it will come to pass. Some research points to the word having evil connections, while others say it is neutral.

When I think of the word wish, I have to look at what it means. Nobody prays and asks God something through a wish. When we wish, we are speaking to anyone who can help us get something done. Any spirit can answer, and I think that is why when there is a wish in movies, it is usually linked to a dark storyline.

Wishing is wanting something for nothing like magic. The concept of a wicked wish is interesting, but if you look at what people wish for, it is often for their personal benefit and desires, regardless of the truth around them. It will always be wrong to wish for something that is not yours.

To use wishing to steal from others is wrong. Nothing good, holy, or righteous can be gleaned from that. But the truth is, you don't need wishes to get most of the things you say you want, but you do need to understand the promises from God. We are all going to die someday, and only Yah knows the timing. Although we may want something to change, simply wishing it changed is not the ticket.

If we want to lose weight, we will have to diet and exercise. If you want to keep weight off, there is usually a lifestyle change and not just a temporary change. It is a mindset change. Similarly, prayer requires you to expand your belief. It is about more than being lucky; it is about knowing you are loved. Knowing there is a purpose for your life and you are here for a reason.

When you realize you are not here on earth alone, but you have the Creator of the Universe fighting with you and who loves you, you are empowered to dream. You can Dare to Dream again. You can see life for how it can be and not limit life to what it has been for you anymore. We cannot change the past, but God has a way of helping us through the past.

It takes guts to believe you can be something others you grew up around weren't. For the slave, it was hard for some of them to imagine that their children would be free. For some, they became comfortable with the dysfunction. Others, who could still dream, had to see a future bigger, better than how they weren't currently living.

What Do You Believe - Embrace Your Crown

I imagine it was difficult for many to decide how they wanted to live their lives and how they would endure the constant oppression. The evil works committed against certain people and the unspeakable trauma many face today can short-circuit dreams. It can make people feel they cannot go on any longer or succumb to the lifestyle around them to survive.

Not everyone who chooses a hellish road in life wants to do so. Many argue if their upbringing had been different, there could have been something different. Was it the environment or the "ghetto" in them? If you take a child out of the ghetto, in that they never lived there, do you think their viewpoint on life could change?

When we are shaped in an environment of oppression and taught the damaging effects of it young, it will play on how we see the world. How you respond is where people differ. Some will get angry, others will become smarter, and then some will adapt and assimilate to survive.

The Bible tells us not to lean on our own understanding because not all roads lead to places we want to be (Proverbs 3:5). All roads can look appealing and promising for a season, but many roads lead to an early death (Proverbs 14:12). You can believe in nothing and be a walking shadow of who you used to be when life gets hard. It was never meant to be that way, but for many, it becomes that way.

Lots of people walk around hoping to feel nothing because dreaming seems too dangerous.

Believing for greater if you are going to be disappointed seems foolish, and wishing at least puts your expectations in the right place. But this is a defeated mindset. This is a negatively charged mindset, and it doesn't give constant power.

We have to Kick Negativity if we really want to overcome unbelief. When we are struggling to believe and find our value, we can be tempted to get negative. To talk about this or that isn't going to work. To believe we are going to fail because everyone else did. To think I can't because we don't see a reason to believe we can.

I want to encourage you you can change your world when you are willing to expand what you believe. When we are only believing for little, when it comes, it doesn't reassure hope. It doesn't bring the gift of believing for more but makes us limit God when we see our wishes fall to the wayside. But wishes are not how you pray or speak to God. He wants your faith with action. Wishing can require nothing but for you to speak it and pray someone else does it.

The Father doesn't need people, but He made it to where he uses people to give to one another on earth. Love is shared between people and we help to point others to the invisible love we cannot see. The Bible says how can you love Yah, who you cannot see, if you won't love the brother who you can see. As humans, we do require the love of other humans to survive.

Our love for each other is not only good for us, but it helps others see God in the earth. How we treat each other means we are like Yah. Being a child of God means we are loving and are like his nature and character. To be like Him, we have to take courage because that could also mean suffering like Him.

To achieve what we want in life requires us to have faith and power. No one knows the value of God like those who have had nothing and gained the world because of the Presence of Yah. When we realize where we could have been or should have been, we see the greatest need for God.

It is in our weakness that God is made strong (2 Corinthians 12:9-11). He helps us to be brave to face the uncertain situations that will come when we step into our dreams. For some of us, it is getting a college education, others getting married, and for some, starting a new business or career. All of these life changes require courage and your ability to believe in the greater.

We can all be blinded by circumstances, events, and things happening now that make us doubt our future. I want to encourage you to open the five gates to overcome unbelief because when we live with them closed, we live beneath our potential, and we are not sure of what needs to be brought into focus. If you have been afraid to dream, you might never start the business you should.

If you were hurt in your past and now you don't want to love again, you might feel contentment with being alone or, worse, being in an unhealthy relationship because you cannot believe for greater. Not believing in what God promised you is dangerous. It not only cost you but those around you, too. You are not living just for you but for the legacy and purpose God wanted to bring to earth through you!

It is work to unpack everything within you. It takes focus, determination, and clear direction. I want to dedicate this book, Embrace Your Crown: Open 3 Gates to Sharpen Your Focus, to help you dive deeper into the you you were meant to become. These gates, Adjust Your Focus, Remember What You Did Before, and Put It All On the Table, will help you supercharge your life. It is time to zero in on where you need to go and determine a route to achieve your destiny. Let's open the first gate.

Thinking Points!

A. What are you believing for?
B. What is a goal that you want to accomplish in the near and distant future?
C. Do you feel you need magic to change your life?
D. Have you been guilty of making wishes instead of making prayers to God?
E. Have you only prayed about the simple things and held back the more complex questions or requests?

Now, I want you to do the Self Check-In to *Embrace Your Crown*!

I. Let's Check You In!
   A. Situation
   1. Have you been open and honest with God about what you need Him to do for you?
   B. Change
   1. If you have been asking for something and not seeing it, is it possible you are wishing and not responding to your prayers with action?
   C. Endurance
   1. When we have prayed for

something that did not happen, it can be tempting to do things yourself. Be encouraged that if your situation could have been fixed by you, it would be fixed already. You have been trying to change it already, right? How has that worked?

D. Persevere
1. If you feel like you have been waiting long, it can be hard to maintain patience and confidence. Remember that ill-gotten things come at a penalty. It comes with heartbreak and incredible risk. Better is a little with peace of mind than more without peace.

E. Acknowledgments
1. No everyone who looks happy truly is. Answered wishes aren't always a happily ever after in fact they often come with a price. Making deals with the devil will never be a good deal and will always costs more than you want to pay. Sin for a season is sweat until the reaper comes to collect. The devil is a liar, but the Lord is the Truth, the Way, and the Life.

F. Re-Purpose

1. When you are waiting on God, or working toward your answered prayer, it is good to connect with other like minded people. When we are in connection with others the wait doesn't feel long, and the time spent is enjoyable. When we slow down, we can take in the sights and explore every area of our lives with intention. Remember to slow down and smell the roses along your road to living your purpose.

G. Help?

1. If an aspect of this chapter was difficult and you want to talk about where you are, please do. Be encouraged; you are not alone. We have free and paid resources to help you work through this series. Skilled coaches, therapists, and speakers are here to help.

Sometimes, we get stuck in a process or want to discover more about what makes us or has made us who we are. Do not feel like you can't linger on a thinking point, question, or chapter. If you need help throughout this book at any point, I want you to contact me and my team. We are a network of coaches, counselors, and prayer warriors ready to help you

Embrace Your Crown, connect the dots, and go from where you are to where you are born to go.

H.	*Embrace Your Crown* Affirmations: Let's make some declarations!
1.	I don't need magic to win in life.
2.	I need the power of God with faith to make divine changes in my life.
3.	I will be obedient and holy, living the best I can with the help of Christ to create a atmosphere for signs, miracles, and wonders.
4.	I will dare to dream again with hope and conviction.
5.	I no longer cast wishes for anyone to pick up and grant, but make petitions toward the Father of Heaven.
6.	Any covenants or agreements I made with the enemy to answer a wish, I cancel in the name of Yashua. I am free from this cov-

What Do You Believe - Embrace Your Crown

	enant by the blood of Jesus!
7.	My hear is confident that the Father hears my prayers and will answer me.
8.	I trust the plans God has for me over my own understanding.
9.	I am ready to *Embrace My Crown*! Embracing who I am and who I was born to become!
10.	I am ready to TRANSFORM and Go BEYOND Change!

ADJUST YOUR FOCUS

THE UGLY TRUTH

"I press on toward the goal for the prize of the upward call of God in Christ Jesus." Philippians 3:14

If you have done the good work, you know why you are here or at least where your focus is right now. Knowing what you need to focus on for the time being is paramount because what you may need to go further down the road can happen when you finish what is before you.

Kind of like how school works. You start at preschool, then kindergarten, on to elementary, middle school, and lastly, high school. There will be a whole lot of information learned, no matter if you are homeschooled, in the public school system, or paying for private education. The quality of what you learned can be arguable, but the process is nonetheless the same.

Adjust Your Focus - Embrace Your Crown

These are the elements of your education you will learn in large part before going to secondary institutions like colleges, trade schools, or universities. Understanding the road ahead will point to what you need to focus on at the moment. If you haven't learned the principles in middle or high school for math, going to college would be dang near impossible to pass. If you haven't completed the previous steps, you won't have the building blocks to get to higher heights later.

Life is the same way. If I skip the lessons meant to function as my foundation, how will I achieve where I should be in ten years? I know it can be disturbing to look at where we are today if we feel it is so far off from where we want to be. We can think, will I get there or if we are dreaming a dream that will not come to pass.

We have to have boldness that gives us the ability to dare to dream, but what about after we start dreaming? How do you keep your dreams alive? How do you keep pressing forward when a degree means four years of schooling? How do you press on when children or a spouse are added to your everyday life during your studies?

How would you feel if you put love on hold to pursue education and your career? Now that you are thirty or forty years old and still single, how do you keep the dream alive that Mr. or Mrs. Right will find you when a lot of eligible people are not available? Some are just as ambitious as you, others have families already, and many have elected to never marry and, at best, are messing around.

K. Lee

What do you do when the dream starts to fade because life is well, "lifing," and your dream is far short of your reality? I suggest that you lock into the dream and adjust your focus. When our dreams are getting distant, it is not that they have become further away but that our focus has shifted away.

When you lock in, do you hold on for dear life because you have determined you shall not fail? Or, do you believe it could happen but have settled with the possibility of it not happening to be okay also? When we give our dreams an out for not coming to pass, we are choosing to consider a life that assumes we are asking for too much. We can believe that it is possible for everyone else but not for me.

I want to ask the question, why do we believe that? Why do we believe what is possible in the earth is not possible for us? How does everyone else get what you want, or better yet, have you really defined what you want? It is easy to see what someone else has and say you want that too. Honestly, if we look at somethings again, we realize we didn't want it genuinely; we just didn't like that we didn't have it.

I have children, I know, if you have them, you may know where I am going. If you have heard that saying your eyes are too big for your stomach, that's a point here, too. Sometimes, our eyes are bigger than our work ethic. They are bigger than our desire. They are bigger than our dreams. We can see something about someone else and really don't want it once we experience it.

My children will see me eating or drinking

something, and the first thing out of their mouths is, "Can I have some?" I reply, "You won't like this. It is not candy, fruit, chicken nuggets, or something you like." Confidently, they reply, "I know. I still want some." I give in to their request, and they say with a scrunched-up noise, "Taste good," as they walk away.

They accepted silent defeat in knowing I was right, and it was terrible when I asked them jokingly, "You want some more?" They reply, "No, no, Momma. You can have it all." Are we not like this as adults, too? We ask for stuff because it looks good. We ordered it, hated it, and wanted to send it back.

At restaurants, we do this a lot. Some of us even ask, "What looks good on the menu?" We can shop by looks and rely on our eyes to guide us, but can't our eyes send us in the wrong direction? Can't our eyes send us to believe things about life, our hopes and dreams that are not true? Can we desire things for our lives because outwardly, they look appealing, but inwardly, they are distasteful?

When we are losing our focus, we have to consider if what we really wanted was what we said or if we wanted it because it looked appealing. We can see a big house and say wow, this house is gorgeous. I want to live in a mansion, too. We don't consider the cost of upkeep. We don't consider paying the maid to help us clean it up or the other costs. We don't see the taxes, the neighbors, the judging eyes, landscapers, HOA, and those that target us because of our wealth.

We only see the house and how gorgeous it

is. We don't consider that the space is substantially more than we need when we find ourselves living alone. Many people who want these big houses don't want anyone in them but themselves and their spouses, maybe. How many children living in these homes turn selfish and never return? How many broken families lose direction because they have distractions that keep them busy from focusing on family?

How many are so busy working to get or keep the house that they miss out on focusing on the people in the house? They wanted the house because it looked good. But their real desire might have been to spend more time with family. Their genuine heart was to show their love and provision to their children; only their children didn't need what they thought they did.

Some people are out here selling their souls to buy things, thinking this will bring more love to their world. How many are tricked every day to have neither the money nor the love? They are in big houses alone or feeling lonely. They are in marriages that look good but are ravishing to the soul.

When we are not clear on what we want, we are not adjusting our focus; we can settle for the outward adornment and not get to the root of our desires and needs. I want you to ask yourself what do you really want. I mean genuinely and wholeheartedly want.

We can say we want to be happy. Very general, right? What makes you happy? Then, many would say I don't know. I just want things to go well. If you pry a bit more, they may say, I want to be in love, to have money, a house, for my children to be healthy, and for things to be good. That sounds really good and can be made so simple.

But how often do we complicate this and add on more than what we initially said? How quickly do we lose sight of what we are focusing on to chase something similar? The biggest danger to your focus is following after a decoy that looks like what you want but lacks the substance. One of the easy subjects to tackle is love.

It is normal for us all to want to feel loved. Having love from our children and family is great, but at times, we can want someone to hug us, hold us, be there for us, and be intimate with us. It is a natural desire that the Good Lord gave, and it is normal to want these things in your life. How do you find or get this love if you are not supposed to look for it, right?

The Bible says a man who finds a wife finds a good thing (Proverbs 18:22). If you are focusing on that, what are we supposed to be doing exactly for him to find us? We can be busy doing other stuff like working, building a business, writing a book, or traveling. Yet, is it possible that these things can also make us unavailable for the relationship when it comes? Will we miss him because we are already involved?

These are legitimate concerns that we don't want to steal our focus away from our goal, which is to find genuine love. I don't want to leave the men out either because they have to do their own version of soul searching. Finding out who you are and where you are going is key to knowing what wife you should select. If you are to find a wife, she is to come and live with you and come under your covering; that means you have to have a means of provision and direction.

Becoming a husband is not easy and no light decision. Any man should consider if they would work their fingers to the bone to ensure his wife and family have a home. They should consider the costs it may take to keep their family together. It might mean he doesn't get his way. That others eat while he stays up to keep watch.

He may have to fast and pray while the family looks to him for answers he doesn't have. He has to be the example that sets the tone for the household. He is the one that people run to when they are in danger, and they trust that he can protect them no matter how big, strong, tall, or short he may be. You are their hero, well, unless you are not.

Your focus in finding love is to find the right woman who compliments your plans and sees value in your decisions. A wife's job, according to the Bible, is to find a man she can respect. A man's job is to find a woman they can love. Both have to find a counterpart worthy of what they bring and worth the challenge to respect or love.

Finding a person that you can both respect and love helps couples work out disagreements and provides the necessary space for cooling off during times of hurt. It allows the two to forgive when things get rough and for us to find solutions when we feel we hit a brick wall. Love is work, but the focus of love cannot be on the things you hope to receive, like houses, cars, gifts, food, restaurants, and trips.

These are social media posts we love to see and fantasize about the man or woman we want. Pictures of people dolled up are not how your wife will be morning, noon, and night. Pictures of him with muscles and well-trimmed won't be what you see all your life. People age, and looks fade. Money can dry up, and real estate can be lost. Things change, and if your focus is not on the same thing, love, it will fade.

So what do you do when it fades? You have to adjust your focus. If you are married or dating, adjusting your focus on love is a necessity. When we are dating we might think lighthardly toward love and marriage. We might be happy with an occasional bouquet of flowers, nice text, and good sex. We might think this makes the man great because he calls you.

But does he respect you? Can he see your flaws and be patient with you? Can he value your body like you should demand for him to? Can you see his response and allow that to melt your heart and reduce your anxiety? Can he be the water you need to calm the fire in you? Will you allow him to teach you, to cover you when you are hurting? Can you decrease so that someone else can walk with you?

For men, can you release some of your control

to allow someone to partner in your vision? Can you hear some of her thoughts to help sharpen what you envisioned? Can you trust her with your wallet, inner thoughts, and plans? Do you have a safe space in her that regards how you feel, even if she might not agree? Can you choose to love her to build up her confidence if it is weak?

Can you suffer to be with someone who might be hesitant to believe when you know for certain you will succeed? In marriage, you are committed, and this is the time when backing out of the relationship should be difficult. If you weren't honest with yourself before marrying, you will have to do it now. The truth, no matter who you pick in life, there will be a challenge to love and respect them.

There will be things they do or say that hurts your heart. Things that make you feel like you chose wrong or could deserve better. Adjust your focus. You picked this person for a reason. You chose to be married for a reason. Have they honestly violated you in an unforgivable way, or are you mad that you are not having your way? Are you mad that you are being made to grow in areas you didn't want to then and now?

Marriage is a commitment to love and should be the safest place for a couple on earth. They should create a strong union. When you are dating, this union won't be that strong because you are not certain if this is the person you need. Our biggest mistake and biggest regret is to treat someone better than their access.

When we play house with people and treat them like husbands or wives, and they are not, we risk not seeing the red flags that would tell us no before the wedding. We could miss the caution signs that tell us to slow down. We can miss the exit when the door is flung wide open because we feel too invested.

I dated someone for a year, and we were engaged, but I didn't feel the engagement was right. I told him that when he asked. I told him that months later, and ultimately, I told him that when I called off the arrangement. It simply wasn't right for me, and I felt bad because our children were connecting. This was the first time, and with this loss, I will not make a decision like this so easily again.

They all loved each other, but I had a huge problem. I could not submit to the lifestyle and way of life he wanted to live. I didn't want a husband over the ocean. I didn't want someone who would be harsh with their tone or words and be condescending toward me. I did not feel free in the relationship to speak but felt forced into a corner to accept his way or no way.

For some, that might be okay, but for me, it was not. I had to pray and fast about my final decision, which I honestly knew long before the day I said, "No, this will not work. I don't want to try anymore." Being honest, I saw red flags long before when he broke up with me at least three or four times. I called it off once, changed my mind once, and then the next no was final.

My focus was thrown off during the relationship. My heart's desire and vision board said I wanted to add love to what I already had, not give up something from my core for it. I enjoy spending time with my children, being present for work, participating in ministry, and productions, but my biggest commitment in life is prayer.

I am flexible in some areas, like work could be cut back. I can change up my schedule. I could reassess my time with ministry, but I had no intentions of changing my prayer life. That was the biggest thing impacting my decision. I hated to live my life on the phone because I felt it was unfair to both of us. It was unfair for our children not to have a hug and present parent daily, that they all wanted.

It was a comfortable pattern I had to choose people who were unavailable. I think, in part, I did this because I wasn't sure that now I wanted a relationship. When I met him, I told him I was building my business and setting things in order with ministry. I had little time for anything else. I was focused when I told him that, but I got out of focus when I believed another narrative.

The other narrative wasn't bad, but it wasn't my focus. When we are not zeroed in, our past and old patterns can creep up and make us return to old things we have already done. I want a relationship that is not built on things beneath my calling but supports it. I need a husband who can lead me in the work I am called to do and be present, more than having a husband with a title.

Adjust Your Focus - Embrace Your Crown

Nothing wrong with accomplishments, having money, resources, etc., but you have to have what you need at the forefront. When you are considering a spouse, consider what you must have. You can make a list because that is an easy way to compare. When we go to the grocery store, we will buy everything if we don't have a guide. Similarly, if we don't know what we are looking for as we date, we can pick up the wrong person.

A love list should be clear, concise, and help you cut through the fat. Not everyone who is interested or matches your situation should be considered for marriage. Just because they are handsome or cute and slide in your DMs doesn't mean you have to acknowledge their interest. Everyone doesn't have the best intentions, and some are just distractions and may not know it.

But you, you need to know it. You need to focus on who you are looking for and seek Yah about it. I can tell you what I write down and ask for I do get. My problem, I wasn't clear enough and specific about what I really wanted or needed. Perhaps what I should have done was ask God what He wanted for me because my list hasn't been the best, although it looks good to the naked eye.

The people you date don't have to be terrible, a dog, a witch, or something negative for it not to work out. You both can be great people, believers, etc, but your paths don't align. If you are not focused on what you want, you can be tempted to adjust your focus and not get clear but shift your focal point.

When someone says they don't want children and you do, don't be tempted to select them if that is a deal breaker for you. I know a lot of people do it in hopes the other person will change their mind, but we shouldn't. I know of a family member whose marriage ended in divorce because the baby he wanted before the marriage he still desired several years into the marriage.

Within a year of filing for their divorce, he was with a new woman and had the baby he longed for. They simply weren't each other's forever, but they played a part in each other's personal growth. They were friends but maybe never meant to be lovers. They wanted to help each other, and the marriage helped them do that. How many of us would help someone because they are our friends solely? For many of us, we want sex, money, gifts, or something to make us want to give our effort.

Maybe this is why dating is so difficult. We are worried about being used, but what if God wants to use you to help other people? What if Yah intended for you to meet someone and care about them aside from what they could do for you? Not everyone you meet and feel a connection with is to be your spouse or a business transaction. The Bible says what you do for those who cannot pay you back, you have done for Him and He will repay (Luke 14:13-14).

I know we cannot save everyone, and you don't have to look out for everyone you date or think to date. However, there will always be one or a few that you notice something great about them. I would suggest you sow your time into good people who can fulfill another part of your life that isn't romantic. People are here on earth for more than being romantically involved with you or buying something from you.

There are people who are in your life for an assignment and to better your life or vice versa. When we give people the flowers they deserve, we are reaping gifts we know not of. In time, you will see the manifestation of your good deed in one fashion or another.

How else are we to adjust our focus? Family, right? We all know they are there but it can be hard to find a place for them. Children seem to be everywhere all at once, and it is easy for them to take over the lives of their parents. Sometimes, I feel my whole life is consumed with raising children, work, and ministry.

Yet, I can still feel I don't spend enough time with them. I can be in the same room with them but not feel close enough. Have you ever felt that your child or teenager was there but not present? I hate this feeling, and when I recognize it, I stop what I am doing and remember why I am doing the other stuff. It is always for them.

When I realize my job is a vehicle to earn money to provide for them, it helps me to remember to have a movie night. When I feel them shifting away from me, I know they feel a disconnect from me that I don't want to continue. Sometimes, we have to work, and we cannot quit what we are doing. We may not always be able to explain, nor should we have to, why we are doing what we must.

Our children are our children and not our friends or co-workers. But creating a home life where they can be comfortable and speak their mind is important. You don't have to agree or tolerate disrespect. Good parenting is setting boundaries and teaching principles that will help them grow up and make it in life.

The ultimate goal we have is to establish our legacy. If you want to help your children grow up and live a life worth living, you must be present to impart your wisdom and guidance. You don't want to assume they will just pick it up or pull it from elsewhere. You want them to know you so they have stories and things to share that exemplify your true nature, character, hopes, dreams, talents, and interests.

If we fail the ultimate goal, to raise children who love us, love Yah, love themselves and others, how great is that failure? How will they learn how to start a business when people are not at the heart of the mission? How can they create a product when they are not solution-driven? What about God? How can they learn to love Him if they have not seen love between their parents or experienced love in their own hearts?

The first teachers of any child are their parents; I have to say that again. They look to us to guide them and show them by actions what life is all about. We teach them with the things we say but more so by the things we do. How we make time for things shows them what is important and what we value. The lessons we teach or skip with our children will be the life we help to create for them and establishes the boundary we have with them in the future.

It is hard for any of us to balance our lives, but we have to try. I am sure we do, but maybe we can see how we can tweak one thing here and there to bring things into full view. Our focus could say this relationship is already toast. What more can I do? Think of what more they need.

When we look out for those who won't pay us back, Yah will pay us back. When we give our children truth, we give them nourishment and power for the soul. They might not like it now, but as they grow older, they will see the value. We are not to water down our instruction for them because we want to protect them from everything.

They will make mistakes, and we will, too. How we teach forgiveness is key because that is what they will offer to you, too. We cannot control everything about their character, but we can lay the foundation. Doing right by people means we can rest peacefully whenever that time comes. We can take mental breaks, vacations, and when the time comes, retire or expire.

We leave our mark on earth by how we treat people, how they remember us, and what they learn and implement from us. Our voice lives on when others speak our story and tell of our history. If no one read your book, your script, or your song, who would even know you were here? In the heart of those you loved and impacted will your story live on.

When we realize and focus on our gifts and talents, not only making us happy but also allowing us to be a light in a dark world, we can see that our picture is much bigger than we imagined. The focal point at first is to learn and nurture our talents. In our infancy, we might not have much power. As we grow, learn, and mature, however, we will grow in strength.

Our focus must be on growing and reaching the purpose of our life's creation and not just fulfilling our own happiness. We can create our version of happiness and still not be happy. We can have the house, car, children, spouse, and there still be something not right. Learning who you are and reaching for your purpose helps you to focus on the right direction for now. It keeps you calm when things are upside down and reminds you that it is not over.

Life will continue to go forward, and so will time. We cannot stop these two things, no matter our efforts to try. What we do control is what we focus on. When we are focused, we can have a sense of accomplishment when we look back over what we have done and achieved. We might think life is complicated, but it really is simple.

As you make your checklist, don't take for granted the simple things. Being able to have Sunday dinner. No matter if the dinner is expensive or inexpensive at the house, the point of the dinner is to spend time with those you love. If people learn to cook during the process or burn up everything, you

Adjust Your Focus - Embrace Your Crown

are happy to be together. It is hard to think of that in the moment when you are hungry, but it will bring laughter when it is done.

What are you focused on? The journey or the result? The results can deceive us into thinking we are doing well because of what we can afford. It can make us overlook what it costs us. This is how you get the big house with the empty heart. In all your getting, remember to get an understanding (Proverbs 4:7). Remember to focus on what is important, and when the wheels are turning out of balance, adjust your focus.

What is being happy to you? Is it the stuff? Is that what makes you think things are good? What happens when those things are gone? How do you feel if you cannot wear a weave, fake hair, lashes, and other adornments? Do you still see the beauty within you? Or would you cry if someone said one joke about your hair, your skin, or your weight?

When we are overly sensitive about our choices, we need to ask what is creating that discomfort or insecurity in us. What has stricken a nerve that we would normally waive off if we had the weave on or something to help us fight? When we feel vulnerable, we may have to self-assess for why something external has so much power over our internal.

When I hear people make fun of my hair, I can say that sometimes I honestly don't care. I like my fro or whatever phase I am going through at the moment. Then there are days when I feel like crying when people say it is ugly or why don't I straighten it. I dislike straightening my hair because I feel like I should be able to be me, too. My hair is curly, so why should I make it flat to please other people when none of them are contributing to the Krystal I had to build with Yah? I also don't like that it won't revert back to my curl pattern, and I have had to cut it off a few times to restore my hair.

I am still working on loving everything about me, and I realize not all the time will you love what you look like. Sometimes, the things that make you unique or happy to be you might not in the moment. Sometimes, the things we are grateful for can go away, and it is out of our control. Losing a house, car, or job can hurt us, and that doesn't make you superficial.

To like your hair in weave is not a bad thing. To feel you want makeup to be your best self is also okay–if you can take it off and love yourself. The biggest focus you should have concerning you is to be able to love you. To love you when you are up or down. When you have weave in or if you don't. When wearing make-up or when you are not. Some may say, but if I take it off, people will judge me.

The world has become so hypercritical of the outward appearance that it makes selling your soul and giving up your mind about what is beautiful fake. Most of the images we see are fake boobs, fake butts, fake hair, fake nails, fake beauty, fake genders, and even fake images built with AI. We say we are a real woman, but so many of us are fake or built on fake expectations. We have to challenge this, or we will welcome a society where everything looks perfect "pretty" and the ugly truth goes undetected.

We don't have glass faces or skin that doesn't age or crack. We get wrinkles, things sag, and yes, we grow old. It is a gift to grow old, and now even twenty-year-olds wear gray hair, but older women die it black, red, or any color. We have to love who we are and allow the shifting sand to be a reminder that we are here now. An alive dog has more life than a dead lion (Ecclesiastes 9:4).

You are worthy of love no matter what it looks like. You are beautiful not just by what you look like but by how you treat people and how you treat and love yourself. How you acknowledge Yah, the one who has created you. You are more than a body, a pretty face, or a shell of a person. You are a living soul brought here for a reason and a season.

You have to remain focused and get past the distractions that will tell you nothing about you matters. That would try to convince you that your dreams are not possible. That what you think about is stupid or not real. You are bigger than your dreams, and your history is longer than your breath. You are eternal, and you have no beginning and end in Christ (John 10:28).

Thinking Points!

A. What areas within family or love do you need to sharpen your focus?
B. We are social beings, who is your support group that you can connect, fellowship, or grow with?
C. Are you making time for the people who matter most in your world?
D. What are your relationship goals and are you taken inventory of how you are being treated or treating others in your relationships?

Now, I want you to do the Self Check-In to *Embrace Your Crown*!

I. Let's Check You In!
  A. Situation
    1. What is the status of your relationships? Are they healthy, dying, toxic, or non-existent?
  B. Change
    1. How are you preparing for the one you are praying for? If you are married, what are you willing to do to positively impact your marriage?
  C. Endurance

1. Relationships are work but also a privilege. We all need someone to be in our corner and our children are our biggest fans when they know you. They want you to win and they will have a heart to give when you help them learn compassion. You are setting the tone for how they will have relationships in the future.

D. Persevere

1. When relationships dry up or become strain, it is tempting to give up on them. For you to write them off as gone and move on. Some cases this is true, but not all. Sometimes you have to remember what brought you two together in the first place. We don't choose our family all the time, but we can choose how we interact with them.

E. Acknowledgments

1. We can not control how people treat us but we can limit their influence. We can make a active choice to live in reality and acknowledge that we will not be perfect and remove that requirement from others. Some

deal breakers can be trivial, remember to focus on what is more important first.

F. Re-Purpose

1. If you don't know what kind of relationship you want or the one you have, look at how they treat you. Do they work with you? are they go-getters or non-starters? Have the person proved to be reliable and dependable? This is a short list and it doesn't mean they will do it, but should they, great. We can have a off day too and miss a lot of them. Remember to take a average and get to know someone to determine what choices you want to make concerning the relationship. Nothing is too hard for God, but something He won't fix, you have to know the difference.

G. Help?

1. If an aspect of this chapter was difficult and you want to talk about where you are, please do. Be encouraged; you are not alone. We have free and paid resources to help you work through this series. Skilled coaches, therapists, and speakers are here to help.

Adjust Your Focus - Embrace Your Crown

Sometimes, we get stuck in a process or want to discover more about what makes us or has made us who we are. Do not feel like you can't linger on a thinking point, question, or chapter. If you need help throughout this book at any point, I want you to contact me and my team. We are a network of coaches, counselors, and prayer warriors ready to help you Embrace Your Crown, connect the dots, and go from where you to go.

Dr. Krystal Lee

H. *Embrace Your Crown* Affirmations: Let's make some declarations!
1. I will spend as much quality time with my children as I can.
2. I will select a spouse based on what I must have and not focus as much on the smaller details.
3. If married, I will learn to discover new things about my spouse each day.
4. I will give compliments to those I love and acknowledge their efforts in my life.
5. I will take inventory on how I treat myself and what i permit

6. from others.
6. I realize I don't have to be fake to be real. I can be loved being me.
7. I am good enough! Through Christ who strengthens me I can establish a legacy.
8. I will recall the reason behind my decisions and learn my motivations.
9. I am ready to *Embrace My Crown*! Embracing who I am and who I was born to become!
10. I am ready to TRANSFORM and Go BEYOND Change!

Action Points:

- What are your stumbling blocks?
- What are Your distractions?
- What demotivates you?
- What Problems make you doubt your purpose?
- How can You Sharpen Your Focus?

Adjust Your Focus - Embrace Your Crown

REMEMBER WHAT YOU DID BEFORE

Over Come Temptation

"For it is better to suffer for doing good, if that should be God's will, than for doing evil." 1 Peter 3:17

Living life means you are going to develop learned behaviors. It is hard to see your age tick up year by year and not learn a thing or two about life. We learn by seeing the results of our actions and learn what works and what doesn't. Who works, and who doesn't?

Yet, there are times in our lives when we can get positioned with a question that we know the answer to, but there is a temptation to change course. To reply differently because we may not like what we see or have been experiencing. We know that stealing is wrong. However, is it right to feel robbed?

Is it right to see what you believe seemingly

dwindle to lesser importance than the ways of others who seem to excel more than you? When we are dealing with the distraction of having less and needing more, we may be tempted to respond differently to a problem we have the answer to.

What would have been an easy no becomes a hesitated no. What should not play into our hearts or minds can start to keep us up fantasizing about how things could be different if only. If only we can overcome temptation. These dangerous openings can lead us to lose the focus we once had on the road.

Release Pain is a book I recommend you read to explore more about the six areas of how the devil gets a stronghold in our lives, witches and demons included. This book will help you overcome the enemy's attacks and restore order in your life.

SCAN THE QR TO
ORDER: "RELEASE PAIN"

Staring too long at what our neighbor has or what is across the street can start to create a strange desire in us to want more than we need. We can resort to other actions to get it that were not on the table before. Also, getting this almost desperate feeling to make something happen by force sets in.

When we resort to taking shortcuts, we will

soon learn there are none that don't come at a price. The reason we are governed by rules is to keep you on the safest road to achievement. The reason there is a job policy is to show the standard for how you can stay employed. The reason there is a Bible, likewise, is to show you how to live holy.

When we decide to cast off the restraints designed to keep us safe, we can forget what we have done to get us where we are. We can look at our situation and see the flaws, see the need or the desire we still have. Can this make us lose focus on where we are going and understanding the road ahead? Yes. Have you ever asked somebody what their 5-year plan was, and they gave you an answer that was detailed and consisted of several steps?

They would tell you that in year one, they planned to finish their undergraduate studies. In the second year, they planned to get a job to help with bills. In the third year, they will work and go to school but also take on an internship to make their senior year easier. During the senior year, the fourth year of their plan, they hope to finish their degree and establish permanent work through the internship or from the referral.

By year five, they are not expecting to be a millionaire but be on the road to setting up their life that would lead to achievement, blessing, and fulfillment. But something can happen in year one for many. They are going to school and it is not easy. They are struggling to keep up with the work and balance their inner demons. They start to second guess if college is for them.

Remember What You Did Before - Embrace Your Crown

It can be tempting to sleep in on certain classes or think excuses will be sufficient for additional days to turn in assignments. It works a few times, but it starts to wear off. At home, things can switch up to make life harder, also. Maybe you need to earn more money, fix your car, or deal with a family crisis. This was not part of your plan.

How many of us know that life doesn't consult us to see if it can interrupt our plans? It just does. The five-year plan you set in place was ultimately to set your life up for years to come. The focus should be on setting up your foundation. Only there are distractions. As high schoolers, our parents are extremely helpful in keeping us accountable. They wake us up, make us get on the bus, and do our homework.

How we adjust to the work is our choice. How we accept responsibility is evident in how we choose to work. For some of us, we are not learning from our life experiences as much as we are enduring the works of others. What you learn, you can implement. What you watch others do is not entirely learning.

In school, you can listen to your teacher, but if you cannot apply that information or repeat it to get the grade on a test, you will not pass the class. This is why cheating on assignments and tests only cheats you. If you are making it off someone else's efforts or merit, when they are gone, you will be left to duplicate the same results. Your lie will be broken when you fail, and reality will set in.

You will not be able to snake your way out

of everything, but you will be empowered to repeat what you learn. You must realize that every situation you are in is meant to be a moment of learning to apply in the future to make fulfilling your purpose that much closer. We are not walking on the job with no experience, no knowledge, education, or guidance and expecting to be the boss.

Yes, some fall into this case scenario, and many fail or only survive on the backs of others. However, when those team members leave, they are at the mercy of other people. These people are not the boss like they think, but mere figureheads. If your desire is to be a boss you must determine what the job description is to match the need.

We can be gifted positions that we grow into. Shoes that were big, but we have been empowered to learn as we grow. Don't discredit the gift or blessing of being entrusted with a powerful assignment such as this. I know that as parents, we all feel in the beginning, we were not prepared.

We were not prepared to know how to take care of this child, no matter how many books we read. We cannot control what our finances will do to compromise what was set up for them. We don't know who will leave, move on, or die. We have no guarantees that cannot change. What gives us confidence to know we can do it?

What makes us settle into parenting faster than anything else? Spending time with the baby to learn their behaviors. If you want to understand how to parent, you need to understand your child. Every child is different, and yes, there are commonalities, but what we need and how we learn varies slightly from person to person.

Some of us are simple, and others more complex. To not lose one, we have to know them individually and collectively. I have four children. My pregnancy with each one of them was very different. With my first daughter, I was married but alone because my husband was overseas on military duty. Although we divorced, he is a present father who supports her.

With the second one, he was present; we were not married, and after we parted ways romantically, he didn't see her as much, never gave no money, and only speaks to her occasionally online. He also lives outside the country. Then finally, my second husband gave me two sons. With the first child, we were somewhat good. But after we went through several landmines as a couple. Ultimately, we were pregnant with our second son when we split. We tried to get it together, but we officially separated the same month our son was to be born, and I filed for divorce a month after he arrived.

So, no two situations were identical, even with the same people involved. The same can be true for you, too. You can have the same people in your life, but life has a way of showing you how their involvement can either hold you back or push you forward. Remembering to take inventory of what is working is critical to know that your purpose is still on the road up ahead.

For some of us, we come to a fork in the road where our paths can link up with others. The end of the road, or just further up ahead, might not tell that same story. Some jobs you take could be right for the moment, but they lose their importance over time. You realize the glass ceiling is still there, and for whatever reason, you have maxed out with the company.

Sometimes, people can limit you because they love the job you do in your current position and how you support others. Others simply underestimate you or feel you are in the best position for your skill set. Consider if that is true or not. Have you stopped working as hard as you used to because you feel taken advantage of? Have the results changed your work ethic?

If you are getting off track, you have to wonder what is holding you back. What has changed your focus, and why are you still heading on the wrong road if that is the case? Is it that you don't want to hurt this person's feelings?

I know that if someone asks us to do something to break the law, we will reply, "no." Then, there are those who will ask us to do them a favor and bail them out this one time, and that person is a family member or love interest. We can be asked by our child to co-sign on a car or apartment to help them out.

We know to say "no" because we are obligating ourselves to their debt or their drama. We have been building our nest egg for years, and now we are putting it subject to their decisions. If it were a stranger, we could easily say no. If it were a certain family member, we can say no, but this is our husband, wife, child, our best friend, etc. How can we say no?

The question becomes, what is your focus? What do you value? Why did you set out on this road to begin with, and what is the most important thing to you now? Is it important to care for family? Yes. Is it important to show your love through support? Yes. But can you afford this price?

We have to be honest with ourselves and set boundaries so that we may be good stewards. The Lord is expecting us to be good stewards over what we have and what He has given us. When we value something, we focus on protecting it. You don't leave your diamonds out for guests to see. You don't go around telling people what you have in your house when you learn that loose "lips sink ships." My momma told me that, and I know her grandma told her.

Most robberies are from people who see what you have, and they come back to take it. If people don't know, they don't have a temptation to break in and steal. If they never see you with jewelry, they assume you don't have it. But if they know you have it, then you must take precautions to protect it.

When people see that you have a heart, you must do what you can to guard it. The Bible tells us to guard our hearts (Proverbs 4:23). We are not to wear it on our sleeves but be wise about it. In the Apocrypha, there is a book that talks about how wisdom went back to dwell in heaven because of the choices of men to reject her (Enoch 42:2).

Do we reject wisdom when we post our intimate details on the internet? When we post our special dates with our spouse or events with our children? Are we giving up our privacy to be social media famous? What have we exchanged in our lives to prove to others that we are worthy, but their scrutiny doesn't create a safe space for us?

Some of us share our lives thinking others will like and approve. But what if people judge and call you names instead? What if you enter a reality show like Love is Blind, and people dog you out for how you treated so and so? No one knows how either of them acted off-camera. Most of us are not in a relationship or have the knowledge to judge others' choices, but we do.

Why do we subject our decisions to people who cannot give us good advice? When we are lost, when we are out of focus, we can be listening to the wrong people. These people will give us advice that makes us feel our dream or purpose is too far off or we need to wait longer to see the results we are looking for. They can make a five-year plan feel like 10 years. They can make you feel that a plan is a waste of time because life will do what it wants.

Yet, when you look at their lives, they will be in the same place or worse in that time frame. If you allow people who haven't gotten to or don't value what you want to achieve, they will pull you down and not think twice about it. You have to look at what you did before listening to them. What has

Remember What You Did Before - Embrace Your Crown

their advice led to in your life that has made it better?

If you are searching your previous actions with them and they led to nowhere, stop following them. I remember when I was trying to make my relationships work with my exes. Every time I went back to them to work on a marriage that was dying or work to be good parents and loves, we ended at the same crossroads. Our paths were going in two different directions.

Not just in what we wanted but how we wanted to live. I cannot change the purpose of my life or what I am called to do. I am not my own but a bondservant of Yah and under the leadership of Christ. When you realize that you are not your own but you work for the Great I Am. You cannot deviate from His plan and think your deviation will please Him.

Remember when King Saul was asked why he didn't follow the instructions of God when dealing with the king and his things? He was told to kill everyone and take nothing for himself. He ended up taking some of the cattle back, saved the king alive, and shared whatever possessions they had with his soldiers.

When he was confronted about doing wrong, he lied. He tried to blame the people, saying it was someone else's fault for why he didn't obey. Samuel told him, it is not me you lie to but Yah. He knows what you did and why. He judges your actions, not me. His thoughts are higher than mine. I am simply the messenger (1 Samuel Chapters 13-15).

How many are mad at messengers? How many don't realize that as believers, we are not our own? We work for Him and when He says no, He will not change it. If we feel lost spiritually, if we feel empty, the bold question is, have you left his assignment unfulfilled?

Did you say yes to someone who should have been a no? We can be weak as humans and know we shouldn't open our doors, legs, or mind to someone and do it against our better judgment. We know when we are doing it, it is wrong. We feel that dark hole forming and so we cannot enjoy the gifts it brings. Like Judas, we are trying to shed the dark matter from our hearts and consciousness.

Yet it follows us into our dreams, our day visions, and keeps us up at night. We regret the choice we made, and we see that it has stolen our focus. We realize our greed or impatience tempted us to make a poor decision. We can be living with our poor decisions that make us question our focus point now.

SCAN THE QR TO

ORDER: "THE BIGGEST MISTAKE CAN COST YOU EVERYTHING"

For some of us, we have made the biggest mistake that has changed our lives. Read the book, The Biggest Mistake Can Cost You Everything, and see what I mean. We wonder what to do now. You have to surrender your heart and plans to the Master's plan. You have to open your heart and ear to be corrected and redirected from your path. Sometimes, it means losing what you gained by doing wrong.

Paul said he counted everything as dung to follow after Christ (Philippians 3:7-8). He had to leave his post in the military. He threw himself into ministerial training for years. He had to deal with the judging looks and the skeptics who questioned if he was truly changed.

For some of us, we have to deal with the words and judgments of people who think our change is a scam. We have to endure the judgment of others because we know what our actions have taken us before. We remember what it felt like to allow others' judgments to lead us astray. Now, we are more committed to focusing on the voice of God above all other voices. We are not going to let them push us out of the will of Yah like before.

It is a vulnerable position to be in the valley of decision. To realize this is the moment where your life will change and things may not be the same when you come out of the valley. You may have to cut relationships, leave positions, change career goals, or behaviors that are long conditioned within you.

When our loyalty is strongly aligned with a person over the area of focus, we can shift, not realizing it at first. But the writing is on the wall. If you were told something that is to your benefit and is a righteous move, but you struggle with enforcing it. That would be the first tail-tail sign. If you meet a person and you don't have peace about them. That is a sign.

If you were offered a job, that would mean you stopped school, or you gave up on the plan with no clear direction of getting back on track; it is a sign. When we are trying to force a round peg through a square, we learn that we are fighting more for the person or situation than what we set out to do. Our energy may be constant, but our focus has changed.

We used to focus on the five-year plan. Our results can be growing, but if they are not as quick as others feel they should be, we can be tempted to jump the boat. If we feel we are working too hard for our goal and the goal no longer holds the value, we can be lazy about following the same course.

If going the initial course means the person we just met and like won't be in the picture we updated, we are tempted to abandon the idea or feel the vision has shifted. The question I want to ask is, do you think marrying would mean you lose sight of what you were on course to achieve, and that be the will of God?

Do you think all the work, growth, deliverance, and peace you had before was meant to be disrupted by this person or job? Do you feel you are working for your purpose or working to be with what you are choosing? The sooner we look at our work, the clearer our focus can become.

We can start off on a journey to walk alone, and the right person should come to support that effort. Your position should teach you a skill on the job. The business should prepare you to deal with what will come next. Your relationship should challenge you in a healthy way to become more like Christ. Your dreams shouldn't die because of marriage; they should be easier to establish.

We shouldn't look at life challenges as subtractions but ways the Father can turn these situations to add to your life. When we have the right people and situations in our lives, no matter if they feel challenging or not, we should ultimately complete the initial assignment to become more like Christ. We will have ups and downs, but we should not lose out on what we planned because we are trying to bring someone who cannot walk with us.

Sometimes, we might start off with someone that we quickly realize they are not meant to leave our lives, but they cannot travel down this part of our lives. For married couples, you might be a minister or pastor, but your spouse is not. They are not called to the same assignment as you but are here to support you.

We can want to make them a co-pastor or give them a title so they don't feel left out, but this could be a grave mistake. We must ask the Father for their assignment or position in the Body of Christ and not in the organization of our church. If you are the assigner of titles and positions and not Yah, you will be growing an ineffective church because your obligation is to the people and not to the Father.

I know the people may want to see these

power couples or presidential-type arrangements in the church, but this was never the way of the church. There were many saints that wrote the bible or wrote about people in the Bible who did not have a spouse who had the same assignment as them. Deborah is a great example. She was a judge and prophetess. She was consulted by military men for her help and she gave it (Judges 5:6-7).

Her husband didn't go with her and try to use his gifts or talents. We don't even know what he was gifted at doing because it wasn't mentioned in the Bible. It only says she was married. For some of us, the person we walk with or sleep with nightly isn't meant to go through the same door as us.

When we pray, not every prayer you make should be with your spouse. Sometimes, it needs to be you and Yah. Just the two of you spending time and not a community event. For some of us, we only pray at church. We only lift our hands or read the Bible on the screen at church. This, too, has to change if you want to sharpen your focus to achieve your purpose in life.

You have to look at what you are doing and what you know you were born to achieve. Every one of us was born with an assignment and purpose for living. We have community missions and singular ones. We have to work out our own soul salvation (Philippians 2:12). Some of us, our co-workers won't be able to get the same promotion as us. We know their skill level is not the same, but we don't want to hurt their feelings.

To that effect, we tell them, "We are going to get promoted. We are going to do this or that," but what if your block is because you are trying to bring someone who is not on the same page with you? What if you are not bringing dead weight, as some would say, but you are being a greater influence on their life's direction than they have over their own purpose?

With good intentions we can push people to do what we do, only they are not us. They try to walk in our shoes, and they struggle in ways you don't. Some of us have siblings who grew up in the same household with the same parents, and yet one can be incredibly gifted in an area and the other has no skill set at all in that area.

This is not because one is greater than the other, but because the two serve different functions. We are not all to walk in the footsteps of our parents. Do you know the oldest would walk in the father's footsteps and inherit his wealth as a cultural custom? The younger children would have to find their position elsewhere or be at the mercy of the eldest.

Then, there are times when the younger is selected, like David, to step up for the family. Every family has a pillar, a Joseph, called to lift up everyone. If you are that person, that means you must make it so that your family can see the road ahead. It is a heavyweight when you are unfocused, for sure. When you are not clear on why you must endure, you can be tempted to give up.

One of the hardest things to do is to motivate and carry people who don't want to be carried. We cannot change the choices of others, but we can choose how their choices will impact our lives. Our focus cannot be to save them from their choices but to set the example they need when they choose to take the road.

Joseph could not help his family by staying with them. Although it was shady how his brothers sold him into slavery, that was turned to his good. It was made part of Yah's plan to provide for his family later in life. Other people's choices can look unfair and be cruel, but in the hands of Yah, they will still work for your good.

Your focus cannot be on the pain caused by other people's choices. It must be on the willpower of Yah to help you win, no matter the circumstances. When I first started doing events, the attendance was staggering. Sometimes, nobody showed up. Another time, two besides my family. Then again, 5 in person and about 15 to 20 online.

I thought of quitting, but I got the feedback, and I saw the growth and how it impacted people's lives. I got to thinking, if one soul repenting and coming back to Yah made all of heaven rejoice, the angels, Jesus/Yashua, and God, could one of them be the one that caused a party in heaven (Luke 15:10)? Can 1 of them be the one He left 99 to receive back to Him (Matthew 18:12)?

Though some would argue my attendance was small, it was the seed I needed to press on. I know what God can do with one person. I am only one person, but I had a team who would give their time to make my food spread, another to run my presentation, and a third to help set up books and things. All these people were given their time with no expectations, an I pray the Father blesses them for it.

    We can keep asking for a group of people to impact but quickly dismiss those right under our noses. We can overlook the few thinking the mass amount is what we need. I have seen more people do greater work with a few than the multitude. Yah always does great works with a few rather than a large group so that He gets the glory.

    I stopped looking at the numbers that would bring discouragement or signal failure. I started to refocus on what was most efficient and had fulfillment. I learned that the few faithful are better than the thousand window shoppers. You give me a handful of people who are serious about shaking up the world than thousands who will only criticize our efforts any day.

    I started to realize that what I was building wasn't a business but a ministry. My heart wasn't to make money or quantify my attendance but to see how I could truly serve. I wanted to put my focus on something other than the numbers or the money. I needed to put the success of this event on the effort and momentum I needed to build to really do a great work with this ministry.

    I am not a preacher or a person trying to launch a church. However, I know the gift and am starting to embrace the ministry I have with books, helping families, and encouraging people through information and spiritual growth material. I want to find those who are intentional in putting their heart, mind, will, and money into what they desire to change.

I have people call me through the non-profit TUG Outreach INC, asking for help. I realized they don't all know what they need. They see their problems, but what they ask for shows they are missing something fundamental. Yes, they can be homeless now, but why are they?

SCAN THE QR TO

SUPPORT: "TUG OUTREACH INC"

Yes, they can be sick now, but how? Yes, they can have a dying parent with a terminal illness, but where are they? Where is their commitment to sacrifice their sobriety to be there for someone who is sacrificing through pain to be here for them? You see, not everyone wants to be made whole. Not everyone wants to transform their lives, but they all want change. I can only pray for what they are believing and will do the work with God to make it happen.

We can send demons away, but they will return if they haven't decided to change their lives (Matthew 12:43-45). Making a life change requires surrendering to the guidance and Word of God. If they are not willing to do that, they are still in love with the demon that is robbing them blind. Yashua sets the captive free, but only if they come to him for deliverance (Luke 4:18). Free people can make the impossible possible because Christ is working through them (Matthew 19:26).

I love how people like Marcus Garvey were able to coordinate and organize people to make effective change. I wonder sometimes, when I look at the state of our communities, why we don't seem to advance forward, although we have more. He had a dream and the ability to teach that dream to others. He wrote newspapers and spread that information to the communities he wanted to change. They all gave something on a regular basis that allowed him to buy a ship!

He knew how to dream and organize to make it happen. He would celebrate the select few who gave financially and make them shareholders in a vision they now shared. He was a dangerous man when it came to change. He had hundreds of black men dressed up and looking like royalty marching the streets in perfect formation. He was not teaching robbing, stealing, killing, and you are a "nigga."

He was teaching them self-respect, enriching them to see and embrace their power. This was what made him dangerous. He wasn't a broke black man with no power. He had resources and what looked like an army that supported his decisions. He was non-violent, but that didn't matter. People thinking like this will disrupt systems and tear down strongholds. "Love" will destroy the yokes.

This man was terrifying, so much so that the US military made a plot to discredit him and deport him penniless to Jamaica. They stole the ship, all he received through the mail, and brought up false charges of mail fraud to justify deporting him.

He has been a great inspiration and example for what I hope to achieve through writing and publishing books. I plan to have a select few who would support this ministry of writing and creating informational content to impact families, businesses, and communities. We can see powerful changes in our lifetime with pledges suitable for individuals, families, or businesses of $35, $55, or $75 monthly.

We change and impact our communities by re-educating and empowering the people. Giving the men, women, and children their dignity back. Calling us to return to our foundation, the Rock of Ages (Isaiah 26:4). If you are led to join me or learn more, please scan the QR and consider being part of the 144 Pledge.

SCAN THE QR TO

SUBSCRIBE: "144 PLEDGE"

Thinking Points!

A. How much do you want anything in life?
B. Right now. Do you feel hopeful, scared, disappointed, or blah about the future?
C. What have you done in the past that blessed you or made you feel fulfilled?
D. Do you see how your relationships are making you better or worse?
E. Do you want to transform your life and be open to all changes?

Now, I want you to do the Self Check-In to *Embrace Your Crown*!

I. Let's Check You In!
  A. Situation
    1. You are running low on energy to see what you hope for because of distractions that have you looking elsewhere.
  B. Change
    1. When we feel like our decisions are not leading us anywhere, we can change our path to make wrong decisions.
  C. Endurance
    1. When you are going through

a hard time you don't want to make life choices. Now, is not the time to make large changes. If you started a business, you don't want to get another job, or quit the business. You want to look at how you have been spending your time and be honest of what you have or haven't tried to do. You need to hold on to the vision because some visions are worth working for.

D. Persevere
1. If you have been hiding from your ideal clients and not picking up the phone. If you refuse to go to events or when you go, you are afraid to speak. You are going to need tools to help you get past that roadblock. In relationships, if you want to connect with people, be willing to decrease so you can be lead or heard.

E. Acknowledgments
1. If what you have been doing is working, consider what the problem is. If it is not working, look at what is causing things to fail. Sometimes it is working because you are not speaking, and more of that leads to depression.

Sometimes it is not working because you don't allow others to speak. So the answer might not be cut and dry.

F. Re-Purpose

1. Take your answer and consider what you were focused on to begin with. When we don't know if something is good or bad for us, we need to know on what foundation we should make the decision. If it is based on money alone, that is not the best answer. Like with my event, I had to look at my heart and intentions for the event. Starting a new business isn't just about sales, but building awareness and customer service. Look at all three before you say you have done everything. See if in one area you have done more than another or if one is lacking completely. Remember your purpose, and make decisions to align.

G. Help?

1. If an aspect of this chapter was difficult and you want to talk about where you are, please do. Be encouraged; you are not alone. We have free and paid

resources to help you work through this series. Skilled coaches, therapists, and speakers are here to help.

Sometimes, we get stuck in a process or want to discover more about what makes us or has made us who we are. Do not feel like you can't linger on a thinking point, question, or chapter. If you need help throughout this book at any point, I want you to contact me and my team. We are a network of coaches, counselors, and prayer warriors ready to help you Embrace Your Crown, connect the dots, and go from where you are to where you are born to go.

Dr. Krystal Lee

H.	*Embrace Your Crown* Affirmations: Let's make some declarations!
1.	I am open to changes that need to happen in my life.
2.	I am committed to my goals and purpose.
3.	Anyone I add to my life should be part of my purpose.
4.	I will trust God to move people in or out of my life based on His

	timing and not mine.
5.	I know I cannot control others, but I can control what I demand of others to be around me.
6.	I will establish healthy boundaries to achieve my goals.
7.	I will not force the people I love to go with me if they decide not to.
8.	I am strong and the impossible is being made possible because Christ is alive within me.
9.	I am ready to *Embrace My Crown*! Embracing who I am and who I was born to become!
10.	I am ready to TRANSFORM and Go BEYOND Change!

Action Points:

- Unravel what was buried,
- What did you do before? How did you start to win?
- If it isn't broken, what is there to fix? However, to grow, you may need to improve or maximize.
- What areas of growth do you see?
- What resources do you need?
- What plan must you enact to win?
- How can you sharpen your focus on your needs and limit what makes you slow to advance

PUT IT ALL ON THE TABLE

FACE THE GIANT

"For God so loved the world, that he gave his only Son, that whoever believes in him should not perish but have eternal life." John 3:16

Wow, can you believe it, we are at the last gate! I had to share the power of this chapter with you and how it set me free. I know some of us are weighed down by different things that have taken our excitement or passion to remain focused on our purpose.

We could have been told we would never make it. We can have grades that prove we are not enough. We might have been fired, lost a job, or are facing financial ruin. We look at these things and say how can I focus under these circumstances?

This is not a big statement, but a powerful and

true one. You need to face the giant and know that what you have is stronger, bigger than whatever you face. Remember the story with young David? He was a young man stuck at home guarding the sheep. He had no big ambitions of becoming more than what he was, and he was content with that.

He had time to learn music, chase wild animals, and conquer them. He was good at protecting and shepherding sheep, and he had no problem with staying in his lane. His lane was the youngest of his father's sons. He was not expecting much because culturally, nothing much would be left for him after it passed down from his brothers.

He probably was content with working for the family and never being the breadwinner. Some of us are okay with working to support our families. We are okay with the small assignment we have given ourselves because we are scared to face the giant. We are running from it and hoping it doesn't call our name.

King Saul was fearful of this large Giant that had waged war on the Hebrews. He said he would fight any warrior he had to put an end to a long and drawn-out fight (1 Samuel 17:10). He was aware of the history of the Hebrews. They could win wars they shouldn't have. They could be an easy pray or a long and hard battle, depending on their position with their God. Many lives will certainly be lost.

He suggested something that might have been told to him to do, considering King Saul was already out of the Presence of God because he disobeyed. I am sure word spread that he wasn't the big man he used to be, so the Philistine thought he would defeat him and quickly usher the Hebrews into captivity.

Only Yah had a different plan! How many of us feel like cattle for the slaughter? On every side, we are being attacked or threatened by a big bully. That bully can be bills, debt, romance, statistics, jail, injustice, and the list could go on and on. We are all facing a giant. Some of the largest giants are internal thoughts, beliefs, and worries that threaten to choke out our futures.

Young David was not afraid of this Philistine because he had been practicing his confidence in Yah this entire time. He had to go up against a bear, and he won. He had to go up against a lion, and he also won. He is used to facing fear. Fear, a giant nonetheless. We can be afraid to dream big because we have tried it or we have been told never to believe it.

David was small and young. He had every reason to believe he was not the greatest pick to fight the giant. Some of you might be small. You might be young. You might have less education or life experience. You might feel ill-equipped, but with Yah, you have more power than you know. When you pick up an assignment with Him being for you, who can be against you (Romans 8:31)?

Although it may appear that the battle should be a laydown, why should you believe that? When the Hebrews had to fight for their life several times in the Bible, we are reminded of the power of Yah to deliver! In the story of Judith, we learn that eminent doom was upon them. They were fighting and losing the battle.

A woman, a prophetess of all people, stepped up to the plate to fight for her people. She didn't fight with a sword. She didn't know martial arts. She didn't come in with a seductive spirit or a plan to sleep her way to victory. She was a widow with money, so nope, she wasn't poor. She had land, cattle, and servants (Judith 8:4, 7)!

Sometimes, you can have everything but still not have what you think you need to take on certain assignments. With all the money, land, cattle, and servants she had, none of them were called to do what she was (Judith 10). She had to walk this journey with other women servants. If she had brought men, they would have likely been captured or killed because they would have been seen as a threat.

She came in unassuming. They were interested in her because of her beauty. Yes, your beauty can be used by God to lift up His people. Our looks are not just for catching a spouse but can be used for the war. When the people suffer violence, the violence take it back by force (Matthew 11:12). I got more on that in a second, but walk with me.

She was set to marry the high commander, and she asked for time to pray and fast for three days. During this three-day fast, she was praying for strength to overcome her enemies (Judith 12:1-12). Are you praying to overcome your enemies or have you felt you didn't have any? We do not war against flesh and blood but against principalities, spirits, demons, and systems of evil (Ephesians 6:12).

She was ready to put her foot down, separate herself from her things, and go on a trip to prepare room for her community. She was able to put her own mourning on hold, to do what Yah asked of her and not sin.

This was not a whore mission but a calvary mission. Her weapons were not carnal but mighty to pull down power from heaven to empower her to fight here on earth. She came into this fast, and she grew in strength each day. How many of ya'll know she needed boldness? She needed help!

She was a woman called to do a job most would say was a man's job. But GOD! Yah can use anyone to get His point across. In the spirit, women can work just like men. We can be planners and work in the military to achieve a win in the Kingdom of God. Do you see a pattern? Women prophets were able to win wars!! Deborah did it, and so did Judith. We serve the same God, and He says He does not change (Malachi 3:6). If He did it before, He will do it again!

SCAN THE QR TO

LISTEN: TYE TRIBBETT
"IF HE DID IT BEFORE"

We have others that are here to help advance

the Kingdom of God. The Father has women and men called for His purpose that He is using. I dare say many of us are called to be apostles, preachers, ministers, offer helps, be intercessors, and even teachers. We have a role in the Kingdom of God (Ephesians 4:11)!

After fasting those three days, she was to wed, but she had no intentions of marrying him. She decided this was the day he would die and that the Lord will give her the power to end it all right here and now. What the Father helped David to do with the lion, the bear, and even the giant, Judith was also empowered to do.

In that tent that was meant to mark a marriage and entanglement of her people with this people, it served as the last blow to send them all packing. After she drove a sharp object through the head of the sergeant, killing him and bringing his head back home, the war was over (Judith 13:15)! We read we serve the same God in the Old and New Testament. The same God that took the head of Goliath took the head of this commander.

No matter what you are going through, Yah can cut the head off the beast. He can rip up the foundation of the injustice. He can ruin governments, crash currencies, close banks, cancel debts, and restore people. We serve a God that should make us unafraid of whatever should come our way. "He is walking around His children here on earth," my mom said. He is answering the prayers of the Righteous now!

If only we had the faith to believe it. He said if you have faith the size of a mustard seed, you can cast a mountain into the sea. Do you believe that? Do you believe prayer and calling on Yah can change your circumstances? Do you think your only vehicle for healing is through the work of your hands? Or do you think no hands are needed, and the miracle will be performed by your wishing or praying?

Paul prayed three times for a thorn in his side to be removed. The answer he received to his petition, "My grace is sufficient for you." That thorn remained. He had to decide how this would shift his focus, his belief, and his faith. Will he still want to serve the God that will deliver others but not save him?

Some of us are out here praying for people and we are the ones who are left to deal with a health crisis. We are the ones praying for the finances of others, but our bank account could be empty. We are here feeding the hungry while others have more that they can do or give. We are burning our energy at all ends and praying for relief as more and more gets piled on.

We feel overwhelmed by the obstacle. Goliath looks mighty huge from the ground. Can you imagine a person over 10 feet standing over you and telling you harsh words? Do you know that the fear you face about death, the Messiah, can relate to that, too? The pain we have felt by losing people who we wanted to come on the journey with us who died, He felt that, too.

Put It All On the Table - Embrace Your Crown

We know it is not easy every day to keep holding the cross, to keep walking, and to believe, but we must affix our focus on what matters. We must put all of our efforts into believing in the power of Yah to deliver and do what He said He would do. We must put it all on the table!

I know sometimes we think to reduce the pressure we have on people's lives, believing we are saving them from embarrassment or ourselves. No one wants to look like a fool by telling everyone this will happen, and it doesn't. We don't want to believe something will happen, and it doesn't happen, so we limit what we believe to protect our hearts.

Only anyone who tries to save their heart from God will lose their heart because they don't have Him (Matthew 16:25). We need His power, we need His guidance, we want the freedom He provides. We won't have what we need to keep walking on this journey day after day if we have no confidence in the name of Yashuah. If we have no belief, no faith, no trust in the Word of Yah, we are poor.

We are poor in spirit, we are poor in power, and we are poor in hope. It is the ability to dream for something greater no matter the circumstances that are in front of you. If you feel you cannot dream bigger, you cannot get out of a funk, and you lack faith in something greater than your situation, or you see this as the only way and have justified dealing with the penalty of your actions, this isn't the plan.

What is the plan of God for you? He is not asking you to pay the price for something that He has already given you a way of escape. You are thinking of life with a ball and chain, not realizing that your relationship with God is a gift. I know some would say when you become a believer, you will be "boring," "too safe," "a buzz kill," or "doing too much."

You are going to have to push past the decisions and annoying sayings from those who will judge your deeds through their limited understanding of your calling. I have people tell me that I didn't have to do all of that. I have stayed up for nearly 72 hours once to finish what I was compelled to complete. Sometimes, sleep takes a backseat when we are pushed to move now!

Not everything you have to do in life will be convenient. Sometimes, you will have to work and go to school. You will need to cook a meal at home and be ready to stay after to watch your children play in their school games. They may understand that you have to work, but their heart wants you to be there. They desire your support and to see your love in your actions.

It is not that your children are ungrateful, but they need you to show up for them. Same as you want others to support what you try to do, your children want you to see their activities as important. When you are starting your business, you want everyone close to you to see what you are trying to do. You call them or text them, but some will only buy when they see you moving.

Don't stay too long trying to corral the wrong

people. They will burn your energy and slow your momentum. Our momentum is not created within our family but within the connection of those who can believe with us. We should not be afraid of stepping out and making our dreams come to past by putting one foot in front of the other. Even the Messiah came for the Hebrews first, but when they refused His gift, He turned to others. He gave the precious gift of salvation to those who would appreciate it.

I have a book about leadership called "Why Leaders Quit." I know many people think quitters never win. And winners never quit. I dare say this sounds nice, but it can be a bit of foolery, too. If you are spending your wheels going in the wrong direction, how idiotic would it be to continue down that road? We have to stop making statements that keep old limitations on our future.

We have to reach past our worries and choose to change our vocabulary so we are not fighting against ourselves. If we are only believing in the power of God when it looks like it will happen. When we feel good about His odds of winning the battle for us, we must increase our faith. When the disciples were on the boat, the weather was beating up on the sides, and the water was crashing into them. They awoke the Messiah and said, "Save us, save us. We are going to drown (Matthew 8:23-27)."

He replied, "You of little faith. How long must I be with you?" How long do you have to hear the Word you will win! Everything will work for your good! No matter what is going on, Yah has a plan for your life to bless you and give you an expected end. He is right here, and He will never leave you nor forsake you.

God is not a coward, and He is not afraid of your giants. He is bigger because the earth is His footstool (Isaiah 66:1). Everything here is beneath Him. We must remember the placement of our King. He is the King of kings and the Lord of lords (Revelation 17:14 and 19:16). His Word is everlasting, and no one can erase what He said about you. If He said, He will restore it all to you (1 Samuel 30:8). It is not against you they stole but Him. You, being His child, make it personal for Him to avenge those who afflict or stole from you.

As believers, we don't get to avenge the wrongs of others (Romans 12:19). He gives us the power to defend ourselves but not to act out in rage and anger to inflict pain on others (Esther 8:11). He judges this and condemns it. With Haman, Esther's uncle, Mordecai requested that the king would allow them to defend themselves against those who would seek to take their lives. A king's law cannot be reversed, but other laws can be brought forth to empower you.

Amazingly, the moment people find out you will fight back, the fight is over! Some people assume you won't fight, and because you have already yielded, they are just taking with no opposition. We have to back up the enemy from off what we are believing for and are called to do or protect. The kingdom of darkness cannot stand in the light, and the light not overtake darkness. It must flee (James 4:7, John 1:5)!

What do you need to stand up against? What have you been running from? What are you believing for but also second-guessing? You need to put it all on the table. You need to be honest with yourself and seek out what is holding you back. You need to make a decision.

Will you walk by faith and not by sight (2 Corinthians 5:7)? Are you choosing to accept the Hand of God to guide you through this phase of your life? He says in your weakness, He is made strong (2 Corinthians 12:9-11)! When you feel you cannot do no more, that is when the power of Yah can manifest through your obedience.

He says, "What you have done in darkness, He will bring to the magnificent light (Luke 8:17)." All the long hours you have sowed into your business are not for no reason. All the lessons you have learned will find a place in the hearts of those who desire change. What you have to give, there will be those who need it and will appreciate you.

The question is, where must you go? Have you noticed how some people give their time to their children, and they don't want it? These same parents start to give their time to others, and those same children start to complain about how much time, effort, or money they are giving to someone else. They start to complain because they know what they are missing out on, and they don't like it.

Their attitude is not toward the person, the parent, but toward their feeling of loss. They get angry at their choice but not choosing to judge it means they get more angry. Refusing to release the pain we have will mean we feed into the devil's plan for our lives. Yes, the devil has an evil plan for your life, and he is rolling out his tactics to win you over. Read the book The Devil's Evil Plan. QR Will you allow him to use anger as a weapon to get you unfocused on making the right decisions to improve your outcome?

SCAN THE QR TO

ORDER: "THE DEVIL'S EVIL PLAN"

We can start blaming those around us and not take responsibility for our actions. But it is time out for that. We must focus on the prize, not the smokescreen. It is now time to remove the excuses that don't do anything but delay our timing. We cannot change if someone has determined to do something to harm us. Accept to show the love of who we are, and the power of God can change them. It is not our job to save them, but the Word is their salvation, the same as it is ours.

When we hold more than we should or bear burdens that are not ours or humanly possible, we set ourselves up with an impossible task. We start believing the impossible is not possible because our prayers didn't do something we really wanted. Our prayers didn't keep our son from running the street or our daughter from choosing the wrong man.

But is it the prayer that is the problem? Or

what we are praying and believing should overthrow the person's will? We all have a will, and yes, our prayers can protect people from bad outcomes. Will it keep them from reaping what they sow, though? Does it mean they can keep committing crimes against Yah and humanity without punishment? Will we be able to save our children by trusting that no discipline or consequences is better for them?

We cannot stop believing in the impossible because our children or those we love choose to do something else. We cannot choose to shut down our future because our bosses won't see the possibility in us. We should not shut down and remove hope from the table because we are leaning on past experiences that were birthed out of conditions that don't match our today.

When we are young, we don't have everything we need to rule it all. King David ruled a part of the kingdom for nearly four decades before he got it all. He was a king, but a king with less than his entire kingdom. He had a Word that he would rule it all and even have a king forever on the throne, but at a point in his life, he had to be content with having seemingly less (2 Samuel 7:12–16, 2 Chronicles 13:5, and Psalm 89:20–37).

He fought many battles to defend his people and grow. He had to wait for the death of King Saul because he had a principle not to kill him but to respect the king God chose (1 Samuel 24:6). We are born for greatness, but we are waiting for our turn. Don't get discouraged at this time or act like the prodigal son and demand your inheritance now. Be patient.

For some of you, you are serving under a pastor to learn. You may feel you should be out front and doing what they do because you are better equipped or knowledgeable. Hold on. Sometimes, it is not about the textbook or things you know but about the Spirit empowering you to do the work. We cannot move without His Spirit.

All things are possible through Christ, who strengthens us! But if He is not strengthening us, how much is possible? If He says wait a while longer, my son or daughter, and we get ants in the pants and move forward anyway. Is your focus strained because God stopped working or you got anxious? The Bible tells us to be anxious for nothing (Philippians 4:6).

I know it is tempting to believe we should have more or move faster. Overnight success stories are not truly overnight, are they? They are manifestations that appear suddenly to others because of your consistent behavior. When what you do in private is exposed to the world, people can see the Hand of Yah in your life.

They are attracted to your light and want to get closer to what you have and how you can help them. We are solution beacons that carry the light to the world. We are gifted in every sector of life and have something to share and offer. I know some of us may feel what is left. Everything that can be done seems to have been done already.

Yet, I am seeing posts on social media daily

claiming the first African American has achieved this. The youngest child today did this. The first in fifty years to do this. Why can't you be the first or the first in a long while to do something great? Why can't you win a Pulitzer Prize or receive a Presidential Award for volunteering?

All that there is to life has not been done to the point where doing it again is futile and of no effect. We all have an audience that needs us to win to encourage them to keep going. Not everyone is listening to the teachings of John McArthur, hearing Charles Spurgeon, or registering what Jonathan Edwards preached.

We don't all understand the history or the findings of the culture represented in the Bible. Some of us need a modern interpretation, which is what Paul did for the Corinthians. He traveled to cities and showed them how the great Yah was present in their world, too. He was great with apologetics and could help anyone from anywhere understand who Christ is. But not all believed.

Even when the Messiah walked this earth, there were those who doubted His power and ability. They questioned why they should follow a king who appeared to be weak. He is the King of the Jews, but He is here dying on the cross. Bleeding out of His side, nailed in His hands, with a crown of thorns on His head, and His people looked on saying "crucify Him" (Matthew 27:28-29, Mark 15:24, Luke 23:21-49).

He was a laughingstock at the time. Have

people been laughing at your dreams? Thinking you cannot do it? That you will not amount to much more than you have been? That your dreams are too big for your britches? That you are not enough to accomplish what you sought out to do?

Don't worry, don't lose focus, don't give up. Put it all on the table. Speak what you believe every day. Work in silence if you have to, stay up nights, and see the success in pursuing your purpose. Don't believe the lies that you will fail when you have the confidence you can and will win.

The devil's job is to distract you with situations and people to make you lose focus, faith, and hope. He will throw up large objects to get you to doubt the strength of Yah. Demons, witches, and the devil work in connection to get you to believe a lie concerning your situation. His goal is to get you to self-destruct and walk away from something that is already yours.

Will this blessing come into your life because you asked for it? Will the Father have the house you asked Him for fall from the sky like quail? Will he give you every prayer you have prayed and require nothing from you? It is not about in return, but does any father do all the work for their children and require them to do nothing their entire life?

Will your parents dress you, brush your teeth, do your hair, feed you, and change you all the days of your life? Or do they require you to grow up? To mature and start using the tools they have taught you to live your life. Do they kick you out to do them on your own? Do they dump you in the middle of nowhere and say survive?

No. They start to give you more accountability under their watchful eye and play-by-play instruction. Sometimes, they will watch you put your clothes on to correct you in the moment. Other times, they will allow you to dress and come downstairs for their approval. They will start allowing you to use a fork and feed yourself.

You are a mess in the beginning. As you learn, however, you gain your confidence and increase their trust in your abilities. We are limited beings who don't know the future, but we can trust that they won't have to micromanage our choices after we have done this enough times.

Our Father in Heaven has an expectation that we will mature under His teaching. When Yashua, Jesus said on the boat how long, He meant how long can you be around Me and not learn from Me. How many of us are around people pouring out or receiving what others share, and are not pulling it in? They are not learning from the lessons you provide but choosing to receive the benefit from your actions.

They are using you and relying on your efforts to save them time and time again. What happens when you don't show up? They learn to rely on the tools you gave them to survive, or they fail learning them. When teachers teach their lessons, the students are not paying them no mind. It is not the teacher who is being tested on the material but the students.

In grade school, the teachers are graded based on the student's achievement, but that isn't saying much when most schools are being rated in D and F levels, and the same teachers teach year after year. How are these scores acceptable? How is it that the majority of students appear to be doing well, but on standardized tests, they perform so poorly?

Is it the test, the teaching, or the conditioning? Are standardized tests really intended to test the knowledge of students for what they have learned or what they should have learned? If students should have learned multiplication in grade school or elementary, is it no wonder why so many of them score poorly when they see it on a standardized test first?

I remember state exams being tricky and holding power on whether you passed the grade or not. We were judged on how well we did on these tests and not how well we absorbed material on a regular basis. We were put up against a scale that could be biased, some argue. We could have had a teacher for part of the year or none of the year.

I found one of my children had no steady teacher for nearly 4 months of school. In spite of this, he already knew how to read 99% of the words on his sight word list for first grade. But this was not the school but home. The students who do the best are those who have people pouring into them at home.

The system is not focused on everyone making it, but shaking up those who they have determined by third grade will fill the prison industrial complex. It is a disturbing detail about the school system that should bother any parent. How can third-grade test scores pick out criminals? What is on the test that determines this?

What I like about our Father, He doesn't have a rigged test for us to take. He is not looking to beat us up for the things we did wrong or judge us for things to prove why we cannot change now. He is for you when you are up or down, and He wants to pour into you so you can enter the world each day with the power to fight whatever may come.

To battle the issues of the world, we must spend time with our Father. We must allow Him to be the loudest Voice in our lives. He wants to prepare you for your purpose. Some of us are demanding that God Almighty move quicker and give us what we ask for sooner. We are treating Him like the father of the prodigal son. We want what we want, and for some of us, when we get it, our focus shifts.

He will withhold bad things from us, and He says no good thing will He keep from us (Psalm 84:11). Yet some of us, when we don't get what we want, we call Him a bad Father and seek to get it another way. We answer a question with yes, when it should be no, because we are tired of waiting on Yah.

We are becoming the lord of our lives and forgetting that even the lords who don't serve Him still answer to Him. The kings of this earth still have to obey the King of kings. No one is free from the Hand of Father Nature. He created everything on this earth and beyond it. He knows the secrets to life that we are trying to find out.

He says I Am is His name because everything we need to know and want to know will point to Him (Exodus 3:14). He truly is I Am. He is the reason we breathe, the reason we have all that we do, and the reason we should want more. Through His Word and by His Spirit, we learn and know all things (John 8:58, 1 John 2:20).

When we start to live a me-focused life, we lose focus on what is important. We lose our first Love. We lose love in what we do, and we do things out of habit. We are a slave to sin, to pain, and to lack. Having things don't make you rich. Having love, power, and a sound mind does (2 Timothy 1:7).

When we are free, we can learn what we don't know. When we have power, we can move our bodies, use our minds, and implement our skills. With a sound mind we can have hope to believe beyond where we are. We can see beyond the trees in the forest and understand how things in our lives can change.

We are not hopeless, left with no comforter. He sent His Spirit to empower us and give us the ability to believe in hope; He will not leave us comfortless (John 14:18). We can trust His name and power to lead us through every valley and mountain. We can believe in the God who won battles for people who should have lost.

The same God who made a way for the Hebrews out of Egypt by parting the Red Sea is alive and here walking with you (Exodus 14:21-29). The same God that beat a nation of ten thousand men with three hundred men is here (Judges Chapter 7). The same God that caused walls to fall that were thick by walking in silence and playing a trumpet on command is here (Joshua Chapter 6).

The one who fought the battle for Josephat by confusing his enemies to fight each other while they watched is here (2 Chronicles 20:15-30). He is the same God with a powerful testimony of His great works on earth. The Bible doesn't hold them all. You and I can look back on what He has done for us thus far. We can see how He has been a bridge over troubled waters.

How he took enslaved people and gave them a way of escape. He is the same God that allowed blacks and whites to share bathrooms, pools, stages, restaurants, theaters, music, politics, and worship halls. He is the equalizer (Proverbs 16:11). He is the great protector who can defend you in plain sight. He will give you a way out from under your oppressor and have His mercy cover you as others hope to watch you squirm under pressure.

When those around you hope to see you act out of character and you stand strong in your convictions, you prove the power of Yah. When you can focus with the storm raging around you, you are doing a great work for the Kingdom of God. We are to be ambassadors who point to the power of God (2 Corinthians 5:20). In our everyday lives, we are to represent Him.

In how we raise our children, lead our business, and leave our legacy, we are to represent our

God. We are able to achieve anything we were born to do when we put our faith on the table. When we trust in the God of our Salvation or allow His Word to be our saving grace, all things are possible. I challenge you to see where your faith is today. Where is Yah leading you as you read this chapter? How will He shift your direction, thinking, or heart?

Yield to that direction and be filled today. To embrace this change, we will Transform and Go Beyond Change. Journey with me to the close of this powerful series.

Thinking Points!

A. Have you been praying safe prayers and only speaking allowed what you are making happen?
B. Is hope and faith evident in your life today in how you speak about the future?
C. What or who are the giants in your life that you need to face?
D. It is not uncommon to feel under estimated; is that your sentiment today?
E. What has the Father did for you before that you need Him to do again?
F. What have you done to advance in life, on the job, and in your spiritual journey that you need level up?

Now, I want you to do the Self Check-In to *Embrace Your Crown*!

I. Let's Check You In!
  A. Situation
  1. When we have been waiting for what we prayed for or worked for to come, we can feel like we should hold back.
  B. Change
  1. Some things that we desire are so large that they will take

time to manifest, but God loves these request just as much as the simple things. Change your mindset if you believe there is something to big for Yah to accomplish for you.

C. Endurance
1. When you are seeking something big from Yah, you need to know stories and examples that can keep you encouraged. I want you to find examples in the Bible and in life that will help you work toward your goal socially, physically, mentally, spiritually, or financially. Starting a business or doing something new can be intimidating or scaling your company, but you can level up.

D. Persevere
1. If you are being challenged to dive deeper to level up, when the result of your purpose is manifested, consider what that will look like. When you can see your future it will help you to persevere when you are going through cycles of doubt or unbelief.

E. Acknowledgments
1. People can under estimate you because you are a woman,

small, short, new, young, or etc. You can feel you are missing something or have everything but the assignment is difficult. With God, anything is possible but what are you expecting?

F. Re-Purpose

1. When you have wins in life it is great. We get the encouragement we need to make better choices and to believe for greater. When we feel discouraged, it is important to look at what you have achieved. When we feel like our desires are delayed, we can feel weighed down when they take time. Consider making the time that you are working toward your goal to be the time to perfect your skills. Master chiefs make more than cooks. So become great at what you do. Increase your wealth as a mother, a friend, a business owner, and every part of your life.

G. Help?

1. If an aspect of this chapter was difficult and you want to talk about where you are, please do. Be encouraged; you are not alone. We have free and paid

> resources to help you work through this series. Skilled coaches, therapists, and speakers are here to help.

Sometimes, we get stuck in a process or want to discover more about what makes us or has made us who we are. Do not feel like you can't linger on a thinking point, question, or chapter. If you need help throughout this book at any point, I want you to contact me and my team. We are a network of coaches, counselors, and prayer warriors ready to help you Embrace Your Crown, connect the dots, and go from where you are to where you are born to go.

Dr. Krystal Lee

H.	*Embrace Your Crown* Affirmations: Let's make some declarations!
1.	I am ready to face the giants in my life and overcome them.
2.	I know my strength is in God, so I am not afraid.
3.	I am gifted for my purpose and I will not fail no matter the obstacles.
4.	I will pray and ask for what I

	have faith to believe for.
5.	I am not going to allow fear to change my focus.
6.	I will not try and bring people on my journey who are not part of my process.
7.	Stay focus on your plan, but remember to be patient with the results.
8.	When others offer their opinions about your growth journey, use what is sound advice but don't feed into negativity.
9.	I am ready to *Embrace My Crown*! Embracing who I am and who I was born to become!
10.	I am ready to TRANSFORM and Go BEYOND Change!

Action Points:

- Face the giant,
- Look at your plan for today, 5-year plan, and how you want to move forward.
- Think bigger than you did before, and find an example that supports where you want to go. Think of the grains of sand. How big you can think shapes how much you can or will achieve.
- Don't get scared by the vision, but be determined to jump all in!
- As you are rowing out to see or taking the turn

that you must to win in an area of your life, don't get weary in well doing. You have to press.
- What is moving you forward? What motivates you in life?
- Lock in to what you must to keep you moving forward and don't look back.

Put It All On the Table - Embrace Your Crown

Put It All Together

"Do not be conformed to this world, but be transformed by the renewal of your mind, that by testing you may discern what is the will of God, what is good and acceptable and perfect." Romans 12:2

    I know that the last chapter was building you up, and that is my heart's desire for this series. To build you up and equip you to remain focused on what the Father has for you. He has great work ahead of you. It is not by our works we are saved, but they prove that we are His children (James 2:18).

    It is what you put your time into and believe that proves what you believe. How you live your life and what you value is important to the Kingdom of God. If you want to see your life changed, you must be willing to surrender your plans to His direction. If you want to keep on the road you started and that road is not His will, it will feel like you are fighting against God.

You will feel powerless and know that you are surrounded by people who mean you no good. You will feel trapped and know that the enemy has a foot on your neck. Oppression always tells on itself. It is heavy, dark, and brings pain. It tries to keep you in a low vibration, believing this is normal and the standard for life.

It will make you believe not having $25 dollars is the will of God but never challenge you to be better with your finances. Yes, we all can get low on money. We all can be low on hope, positive thinking, or health. However, what pulls a group away from the pack? What you feed will either feed you or enslave you!

If you continue to put your faith in things that don't work for you, you will continue to lose. When we store things in dirty vessels, we contaminate what we put in the vessel. Some of us are putting our great words, powerful efforts, and desires into vessels, people who have ill intentions. We are showing our hearts to those who are not there to make our lives better.

They are there to discourage you and call your dreams unrealistic. They make you feel that what you want out of life is too simple or little. They tell you you need a mansion or fancy car. They tell you to be well off, you need high-ticketed items and not peace.

They tell you you cannot make it by doing everything right. That living holy is boring, and that you are not going to enjoy life if you play it safe. They say the weak need God, but they don't read enough to know that there is a judgment against the rich who get there by oppressing others will also be judged. They put their faith in their weapons, money, and systems of oppression.

They underestimate the God that is waring for you. The One who takes you out of harm's way and gives you a way of escape. They don't want to acknowledge that they don't know how you live and become so resourceful. When they try to take your food, contaminate your water, or limit your rights, you come up from the ashes.

When you are dead, dead in hope, empty of progress, or feel like all is lost. When others look at your communities, they say it is over for them. How can they survive this? When laws are passed to press you in, to hold you down, the God up above will make a way for you. He will hold back the devourer so you are not afraid. He will pull back the powers set against you so that you can see the light through the darkness.

He is the only way to transform your life and go beyond change! He is the chain breaker and the answer to your every need. He is healing to the sick. He is joy to the depressed. He is a father to the fatherless. He is the mother to the motherless. He is the dream for those afraid to dream. He is the light to those in darkness!

He is the one who sets the captives free. If you have been held back and felt let down time and time again, I am here to point to the one who transformed my life by His power. His Spirit has walked with me when I had nothing and carried me as I have gained more. When I could barely afford to live on my own until I could rent a 4-bedroom home, buy houses, and obtain more.

When I lost my car, He gave it back and paid off the note! When I went through loss, I didn't say it was over! I knew greater was He able to do with my situation, and I had to settle in my heart that nothing was worth losing my focus on His power. I had to trust Him when my life went underwater, believing that He would either give me air or bring me back up in time. If I died, He would revive me.

We can die. We can die to the cares of this world and die to the life of sin (Romans 6:11). We can choose to have life and life more abundantly all the same. We can choose to open the gates to find out why our hearts have been broken and apply the action to overcome it. We can dare to dream that life can be better.

We can choose to understand that we don't need magic; we need power! We need the presence of God to change our lives. We need Him to give us the confidence to dream again. We need him to point us to a road that goes out or through our troubles. We need to sharpen our focus and adjust our faith so that we can walk in the boldness we had in the beginning.

It is to our benefit that we remain focused on His light, power, and presence rather than allow the circumstances around us to distract us. We must choose to focus on Him no matter the money we have or don't have, who is around us, where we live, how we feel, if we are sick or well. When we make up our minds to serve Him, we are going to be Transformed. He makes us a new creature.

He removes the old things and replaces them with the new. He will get rid of the old wineskins so that your new thinking and actions can be put into new wineskins. Your actions won't be wasted because they are being preserved in the wineskin. It won't burst and be lost!

The Father is storing up some of our prayers for a different time. Abraham's prayers are still being unfolded before us. The prayers of Ezekiel, Jeremiah,

Isaiah, and many others in the Bible, we are living out their visions and prophecies today and until Christ returns. We are seeing why Jeremiah was called the weeping prophet.

Yes, times behind us were difficult, and the truth is that some ahead will be uncomfortable, too, but the same God is able to make room for our escape. Apply what you need from this powerful collection to refuel your belief tank. To keep you focused and open to faith. Use this series to help guide and build your faith for what the Father desires to do for you. Greater works are you able to do because your Savior sits at the right hand of the Father.

He makes requests for you and intercedes on your behalf. He loves you and is calling you by His Word to surrender not for His benefit but yours. All those who are heavy-laden He will give rest. Those who are bound, He will set free. Those who will surrender it all, He will fill every part of them. He will keep you light even when the storm rages outside. He will protect you from the arrows by day and the arrows by night (Psalm 91:5).

You can live life without fear. You will be free. You are loved. You have a purpose. Embrace Your Crown and fulfill the purpose set within since before the foundation of the world.

Shalom, peace and blessings

K. Lee

Transform Go Beyond Change - Embrace Your Crown

ABOUT THE AUTHOR

About Author

"God blesses those who work for peace, for they will be called the children of God." Matthew 5:9

Krystal Lee is proud to have authored this book and accompanying course to better the lives of readers. She has a heart to help people in their deepest times of need. She writes because she believes there is power in sharing stories and life accounts, that others can benefit and learn from. Sharing is caring, so she shares stories, ideas, and resources to better the lives of her readers.

In addition, Dr. Lee has authored over 35 books across twelve or more genres (adult, children, youth fiction, self-help, spiritual growth, novels, and more), in addition to ghostwriting and editing more than 20 published works. She has launched coaching programs, web courses, and helped in the formulation of many startup

About the Author - Embrace Your Crown

companies. Her specialty lies in aiding coaches, creatives, and service-based companies in defining their message, brand, unique selling point, client avatar, and generating a sales cycle and structure for her clients.

Empowering individuals is at the core of her work, and she is driven by her passion to continue writing. In addition to being an author, Krystal Lee is a business owner of multiple companies, a consultant, an ordained chaplain, and a speaker.

For more information about Dr. Krystal Lee scan the QR. To engage with the Coaching series and Monthly Meet up Group for Embrace Your Crown First Sundays at 4pm, please use the QR or visit InviteEyc.com and EmbraceYourCrown.com

Resources

Congratulations on completing this book! Your decision to engage with it is a significant accomplishment that deserves recognition. As a token of appreciation, I would like to offer you two fantastic gifts!

Firstly, I would like to extend a complimentary invitation to our online gathering, First Sundays *Embrace Your Crown*. Every first Sunday of the month at 4 PM EST, we come together as a community to discuss topics related to our purpose, families, finances, businesses, and careers. Our group is not a social club, but rather a space for Kingdom-building. We are invested in your progress, and we believe that as you advance, you'll add value to the Kingdom of God.

A bit more about First Sundays! During our meetup we speak to:

Resources - Embrace Your Crown

Kingdom Builders

You are coming because you have a body of people that you need to pour into, but you too need someone to pour into you. Likely you have churches, organizations, or a business. I invite you to come!

Royals

You are operating in your career, functioning in your home, but you need a reminder, a WORD, to lift your consciousness from the mundane things set around you. You need to reconnect with your purpose so you can launch into the deep! Come!

Knights

You are standing in the gap of people you know. You are a giver, prayer warrior, and constant friend for people in need of help. You may not be religious, but you are intent on helping people around you. You seek information and ideas that can help those you love or care about. If someone is hurting and you want to help, come!

Specially invited guest

You are not sure what may be spiraling out of control. There are too many things to count. Family, finances, relationships, job/career or business seems to be falling and you don't know why. You are sinking sand and want to stand. Give us your hand, come!

With your complimentary 30-day trial to Embrace Your Crown, you will be granted subscription level-access. This grants you access to our First Sunday Meetup at 4 PM EST for one month. Moreover, you will get benefits, which includes weekly encouragement, presents, and exclusive invites solely for our members. We look forward to connecting with you soon.

Furthermore, our goal is to help you discover your purpose and recognize your status as royalty, based on His blood shed for you. It is beyond time for you to Embrace Your Crown, Royal. Furthermore, we'd like to assist you in connecting the dots to launch your business, write a book, or pursue a new endeavor. We have a team of coaches, therapists, and business consultants ready to help you fill in the missing pieces to achieve your goals. I encourage you to take advantage of our complimentary Breakthrough Call, where we'll discuss your next steps and identify how best we can help.

Don't waste any more time; scan the QR code for your Free Gift and let's stay connected.

FREE GIFT

770-240-0089 EXT. 0
info@KrystalLeeEnterprises.com

Congratulations!

Great job on completing the third and final book in a three part series! Your decision to engage and read to the very end is an accomplishment that you should celebrate. I have gifts for you and resources that I believe will help you.

Starting my businesses, same as writing every book and publishing, so far 37, took a team and a process. If you are looking to take a journey into your own business or write and publish a book of any kind, I want to share a resource with you: WAE Process and KLE Publishing. If you want to start a business, KLE Business Concierge has been extremely helpful. More details down below.

Lastly, if you want to pick up your next book I wanted to give you a short list of some good books from several genres that I can recommend from my collection. Scan QR or order at AuthorKLee.com

Spiritual Growth:
Bless the Works of My Hands 21-Day Devotional
Release Pain (40 Day Devotional)
The Embrace Your Crown Series (3 books!)
- Open 7 Gates to Find and Overcome Heartbreak
- Open 5 Gates to Overcome Unbelief
- Open 3 Gates to Sharpen Your Focus

Christian Fiction (Novels that Inspire)
Leaking
The Gray Space
The Monster
We Expect Drip, Not the Downpour
The Alone But Never Lonely Series

Children's Books
Put Your Helmet On
The Weight of the Elephant
Loves You
Samantha's Greatest Gift
The Lesson Series for Youth and Teens (10 books!)

Books for Him (Husbands/Sons)
The Biggest Mistake Can Cost You Everything
Rise and Fall of King Saul
The Ecstasy
Over the Fact

Starting a Business: Turn Key Solution: (Series)
- Go From Dreaming to Paid
- Nail Your Sales Goals: Books & Services

Writing & Publishing Your Book Easily! (Series)
- Write Anything Easily (Books & E-Books)
- Creating the Perfect Story (Novels, Scriptwriting, Audio books)

Resources - Embrace Your Crown

If you are looking to launch a business, write and publish a book, or need help automating and expanding your business, I can not say enough about Krystal Lee Enterprises (KLE) services to help handle your endeavors.

Coaching Services: Lee and her Team help people find their purpose and live on purpose.

Writing and Publishing Department: Writing services for Businesses, Websites, Documents, Books/E-books, Production Scripts, and Plays.

The Business Concierge: Offers Small and New Business Services that include Message and Brand development, Client Demographics, Sales Structure and Sales Cycle Creation. Along with Social Media and Website support, and CRM creation and management services.

Production: This department supports Film, Video, TV, Plays, Podcasts for scripting, recording, distribution, and more.

If you are ready to get started with any of these services, KLE would like to give you a special promotional offer of 10% off your entire order when you use the QR code to fill out the short survey. Your promo can be applied to books, courses, and services offered by KLE.

770-240-0089 EXT. 0
info@KrystalLeeEnterprises.com

AuthorKLee.com Creator of *WAE Process*

Explore over seven different book genres, and find something suitable for every member of the family.

SCAN ME

Call or Text:
770-240-0089 Press Extension 1
Web: KLEpub.com
Email Services@klepub.com

It's time to start and finish   **YOUR Story!**

KLE Publishing specializes in helping people become authors. In as little as 15 to 90 days, we can help you develop your books and e-books and publish to 39,000 outlets! We also offer audiobook services.

Write, Edit, Format, Publish
We can help from
Start to Finish.

Explore and learn more about published authors affiliated with KLE.

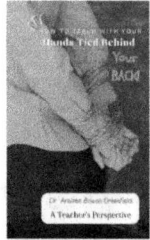

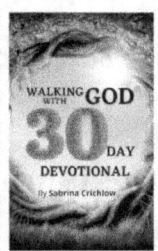

KLEPub.com

www.ingramcontent.com/pod-product-compliance
Lightning Source LLC
Chambersburg PA
CBHW070102080526
44586CB00013B/1161